JADE-SKY'S

PSYCHIC
SECRETS

JADE-SKY'S

PSYCHIC
S E C R E T S

Connecting with your intuition

ROCKPOOL
PUBLISHING

A Rockpool book
Published by Rockpool Publishing
PO Box 252, Summer Hill, NSW 2103, Australia
www.rockpoolpublishing.com.au

First published in 2011
Copyright © Jade-Sky, 2011

National Library of Australia
Cataloguing-in-Publication Entry
Jade-Sky.
Jade-sky psychic secrets : connecting with your intuition /
Jade-Sky.
9781921878480 (pbk.)
Psychic ability.
Extrasensory perception.
Clairvoyance.
133.8

Cover and internal design by Red Mullet Creative
Cover Picture Research by Lisa Scelzi
Edited by Jody Lee
Typeset by Ice Cold Publishing, Sydney
Printed and bound by Griffin Press
10 9 8 7 6 5 4 3 2 1

To Lilbearpawwoman, Golden and Tenfeathers, my true
friends and spiritual teachers. Thank you for your support,
patience and friendship. Even though I am in Australia and
you are in the USA, my heart is with you. Without each
of you I would still be lost between two worlds.

I would like to thank my three children, my family
and friends for their love and support.

To Richard Martin - thank you, your insight
and advice are always so very helpful.

To Stacey Demarco, thank you so much for writing the
foreword, it means so much to me. Your friendship and
support is a wonderful gift in this ever-changing world.

To Lisa Hanrahan and the team at Rockpool Publishing,
thank you for your professionalism and
support in making this book.

And last but not the least, to my Spirit Guides,
thank you for all that you do.

Contents

Foreword

Humans have been attempting to build bridges between this world and 'the other' long before history was recorded. Shamans, custodians of the tribe's spiritual and physical health, communicated with the earthly and spirit world in order to heal and protect their tribe's spiritual and physical health.

Every culture has an oracular tradition; that is, a way of allowing deity or universal energy to speak though them for predictive wisdom. Whether it's consulting the coffee beans in Ethiopia, chicken entrails in remote Indonesia or the runes in Scandinavia, people instinctively wish to know more about themselves and their future.

Consulting a wise seer, the witch of the village or the priestess of the temple was once an everyday event. In complex civilised societies such as ancient Greece, whole cities sprang up around seats of oracular power. Perhaps the most powerful oracle of all was at Delphi in Greece, where it was said that the God Apollo spoke directly through his priestess. The advice of the Delphic oracle was sought by powerful and legendary figures, such as Caesar and Alexander, with whole wars turning on what the oracle had to say.

In this time of technology, science and mass knowledge, people are still interested in developing their intuition or psychic ability and this interest has grown exponentially.

As a metaphysicist and someone who has studied psychic ability and other practical spiritual arts, I find this renewed interest in psychic revelation something worth looking at.

Is it that people wish to hand over the responsibility for decision making to someone else? Is it that people are simply silly and superstitious? Is it that they instinctively feel that there is more than what science presents to us right now? Have these people felt glimmers of this very skill within themselves? These are complex questions but I believe the last two questions provide the answers.

There is no question that psychic ability exists, although I clearly don't believe in every psychic and I am in the majority with that view. While the pseudo-sceptics and sceptics may disagree, the majority of people do believe that psychic ability is reality.* It is a rare person who hasn't experienced a 'gut feeling' that 'something told them' to make a decision, or had an experience of knowing who was going to be on the other end of a phone line before answering. We often call this feeling of inner knowingness, intuition. I like to think that psychic ability is intuition on steroids! That psychic ability is a completely natural — although supernatural — talent that people can be more genetically or physically disposed to. However, these are skills we can all develop. This is what *Jade-Sky's Psychic Secrets* brings to you.

I met Jade-Sky a number of years ago, connecting with her instantly. We had a conversation about mediumship and I found her quiet dedication to serving others refreshing. In a world where mediumship is becoming about 'the show' rather than the service, her humility and egoless way of working was impressive. I decided to have a reading with her and found that she did not use cold reading techniques and that the reading tackled the past (verifiable), present (also verifiable) and the future. With the future predictions she happily gave dates, names and times, and years down the track; over half of these predictions came to pass. We began to work together on workshops and books, not because our methods are similar but because they are different! We believe that there are many paths to the same destination and that this benefits the student or enquirer.

There are many books about psychic phenomena, the science of the supernatural and mediumship. A useful book in this area doesn't just tell a story about the practitioner, but invites you to participate and increase your own change should you desire it.

Psychic Secrets gives the reader a simple step-by-step guide to trying a whole variety of traditional skills. It is also a book that requires joyful action and curious participation. Try the exercises and answer the questions. In doing this you will gain full benefit from what this graceful teacher is giving to you.

I am gratified to see that Jade-Sky has mentioned the importance of connecting with earth energies and the power in grounding with these methods, which is something that I teach and recognise as extremely valuable in development. Shielding and grounding are overlooked in many psychic skills programs, to the detriment of developing practitioners. I liken this to going to the gym for the first time and going straight for the heavy weights — maybe you can give them a good push, maybe you can lift them, but there is a very good chance that you'll damage yourself trying. It would be so much better to have a good instructor, a good level of fitness before the attempt; no one gets hurt and your muscles grow! Spiritual damage prevention is as important as physical damage prevention.

Whether you are a believer in the spirit world or psychic ability, or are someone who wants to improve their 'gut feel', you will find something worthwhile for your time and effort within these pages.

Enjoy!

Stacey Demarco

Metaphysicist, Author, Witch

* Here are details of one such survey: Gallup Poll 2005, http://www.gallup.com/poll/16915/Three-Four-Americans-Believe-Paranormal.aspx

INTRODUCTION

Introduction

Are you interested in becoming more intuitive or want to learn about opening up your psychic abilities? If the answer is yes, you have come to the right place. In choosing this book you are well on your way to opening yourself up psychically. Discovering how to use your sixth sense or intuition isn't about being the next famous medium or a psychic reader in a crystal shop. You can use this skill to help you in your everyday life.

Being connected to your own intuition can help you navigate your way through life with a bit of help and guidance. You will be able to sense if a situation is right for you and your family or if you need to be cautious.

As your psychic abilities develop you will also notice things in your environment that you may not have been aware of before, such as other people's energies and how they affect you, as well as things that you should be looking out for. You may also be able to predict things that will happen in the future that can help you steer yourself and others in the right direction.

Looking into the future or sensing things psychically is not a new concept. Throughout the ages, shamans, mystics, and wise men and women have helped people to get to know more about the spiritual world and how it affects the physical world they live in.

In tribal societies or in situations where there is a strong need to rely on instinct and intuition to survive, it is common to rely on a highly developed sixth sense and intuitive side. For example, hunting for food for your family in the middle of the jungle or savannah becomes a matter of life or death, and to survive you need to be aware with all of your senses. If you feel that something is following you or you get a feeling to go into a particular area it can make the difference between your family eating or you being eaten by predator.

In the modern Western world, even though we may not have to look out for animal predators and we may not have to hunt for our food, there are other things we need to protect ourselves from. We may need to look out for energy predators or people that are not safe for us. We may need to use our intuition to know which is the best way to move forward when making decisions about family, career, health and finances.

Throughout this workbook I aim to provide you with various activities and information to help you to meet your spirit guides, to open yourself up psychically, to see and feel auras and to be able to sense things psychically with your sixth sense.

I know that in my life as a professional psychic medium and as a wife and mother, my intuition has saved me and my family from all sorts of different scenarios — from little things such as intuitively knowing who to trust around my children right up to making serious life decisions about finances and my business.

Sit back, enjoy the book, take time to do the exercises as you go along and most of all have fun connecting with your intuitive side!

COMMON QUESTIONS ABOUT PSYCHIC AWARENESS

How do I know if I am psychic?

This is a question I am often asked. There is not just one thing that will let you know that you are psychic. It can sometimes take years to learn how to predict things at will or to tap into your intuition. Each person is born with their own intuition which means they all have the ability to connect psychically. It is just that some people do not know how to or they are not aware that they can learn more about their own psychic ability and intuition.

When you are first learning about your psychic ability it is good to take note of the things you feel, see or sense that are out of the ordinary. Think back over the years and remember the times that you have sensed things or had a gut instinct about things that turn out to be true.

These feelings tell you that you are using your sixth sense. It does not mean that you have to be a professional psychic but it may mean that you are very intuitive and can predict things or work with psychic energy in some way.

The best way to know that you are not making things up or imagining things is by validation and confirmation. A validation or confirmation happens when you know specific information about a person that you have no way of knowing, or you picture an event and it comes true, or the information you instinctively know is correct.

I often have dreams of things before they happen, premonitions. Why do I have premonitions if I can't fix things or stop things from happening?

A premonition is when a person senses, sees or feels that something is going to happen in the future and it actually does end up happening. Sometimes premonitions can be very disturbing; you may see something that is a disaster that is going to happen or feel that something will happen to a particular person.

It can be difficult to deal with having a premonition when it is about something that is quite traumatic and there is nothing that you can do about it. For example, it is said that a lot of people had premonitions about World Trade Center bombings before it happened.

I have asked my spirit guides the same question about premonitions. I was frustrated because I was continuously having a dream about a particular event. The problem was there was nothing I could do about the event, it was something that was out of my hands and it was in the hands of the authorities.

When I asked my spirit guides about this they told me that sometimes, as hard as it is to see or feel, they give us a warning or premonition to prepare us for what will happen. In some cases you may be able to warn a person or change the event from happening; in other cases you can't. It might just be a learning lesson to train you to listen to your spirit guides and see that you are right, confirming your sense of what is about to happen.

What is the difference between a psychic and a medium?

A psychic can usually pick up information about the person's present, future and sometimes their past or past lives. The psychic should be able to give very specific information to the person by using their sixth sense, that is, through clairvoyance, clairaudience, clairsentience and so on.

The role of a psychic is to help people to move forward in their lives by giving them confirmations and validations about things that have already happened in that person's life. They can also help by giving them information about their future path or past lives.

A medium is a person who can connect with deceased loved ones. A medium is like a phone line between the living and the deceased. It is the medium's job to pass on very specific information such as names, dates and personal details about the deceased loved one to prove that they are still around the person, that they still exist.

I am a psychic and a medium combining both of these skills when I am doing my readings. Not all psychics are mediums as not all can connect to deceased loved ones.

What is an empath?

Empath is short for the word empathetic. You may have heard the term that someone is an empath. It is a common term in spiritual groups. When someone is referred to as being an empath it means that they can feel other people's energy.

An empath can feel both the good energy and bad energy around other people. If an empath is around someone who is quite negative or sick the empath may start to feel that themselves in their body. It can be very confusing for the empath because they may feel like it is them that is sick. It is not until they are away from that person that they may notice that they feel better.

It's important that empaths learn how to ground and shield their energy so that they don't get so drained.

One of my sons is an empath as he will often feel other people's pain or sickness, or will come home from school totally overloaded from all of the other children's energy. I am lucky that I know when he is like this; he tends to be quite angry or defensive or feel very upset in his stomach. When this happens I ask him what has happened at school or who has he been around and it often explains a lot to me. The best thing for him is to ground himself quickly so I get him to hold a piece of hematite crystal (iron ore) in his left hand until he calms down and gets rid of the extra energy that doesn't belong to him.

Why do I feel so drained when I am around large crowds of people?

Sensitive people can feel drained in large crowds; the energy of all the people can make your head spin. You may also be an empath (see question above). Try to take note of what is going on around you when you feel drained. Is it a particular place that makes you drained or is it just the large number of people around you?

Often my hands tingle or feel really hot when I am near particular people

This happens quite a lot to me. Often my left hand will tingle or feel really hot when I am near someone with a lot of energy, particularly healers. I feel this happens because I am feeling their energy and aura.

When you are clairsentient you can feel energy in all parts of your body, so it's not surprising it sometimes happens in your hands.

What happens when I see circles of light floating around in photos or near me?

These little circles of light are often referred to as spirit orbs. They can be seen with your physical eyes, your third eye with your eyes closed and can even be seen in some photographs.

A spirit orb is the energy circle or imprint left by a spirit. The spirit may be a passed loved one who is coming in to see how you are or it could be a spirit guide or just a spirit going past you.

When I see spirit orbs with my physical eyes it usually happens very quickly. I will be walking along and out of the corner of my eye I will see a bright flash of light in the shape of a circle zoom past me. By the time I get a chance to look at it more clearly it is gone.

There are many photos that have spirit orbs in them. Have a look at your photos next time. Digital cameras are so sensitive they seem to be able to pick up the orbs very well. You can also sometimes see spirit orbs in aura photos.

PART
ONE

Psychic protection

To psychically protect yourself involves grounding your energy, surrounding yourself in positive energy and shielding that energy so that your own positive energy remains intact.

In times gone by, village elders or spiritual teachers would teach their students how to psychically protect themselves. The students may have taken weeks, months or years to learn the art of psychic protection. The student would not be allowed to begin to learn the psychic arts or psychic skills until the teacher or elder thought they were more than capable of handling any energy which may be thrown at them both positively or negatively.

Unfortunately for many of us living in developed countries, we don't have a village elder or someone in the community to teach us how to connect with the spirit world and our own intuition. It is left up to us to find our own information out and it can be difficult to know where to start to learn and who to trust.

I want to start with psychic protection. I am teaching you from the beginning about psychic protection as it has been taught to me, and as it has been taught in various different ways down through the ages. Psychic protection is important because it allows you to feel confident and safe when you are connecting with the spiritual world and using your intuition.

Reconnecting with source and grounding

This is the first lesson about reconnecting with your source and grounding your energy.

WHAT IS GROUNDING?

Grounding is the word many people in the spiritual world use to explain the process of centring your thoughts and protecting your energy. It is one of the most important self-care activities you can do. By grounding yourself you will become more relaxed and balanced in your mind, body and spirit.

It is very important for everyone to ground themselves, especially sensitive people and spiritual healers and workers who may often feel depressed, drained or lethargic because of their work, lifestyles or their surroundings.

Physical signs that you are not grounded

Due to our modern lifestyle most of us don't have enough time to spend in nature or to spend time relaxing and focusing on what we would like to achieve.

Any one or more of the following are signs that someone may need to reconnect and ground their energy. (Please note that sometimes there may be a medical explanation for some of these symptoms or signs. Make sure you check out all medical options or reasons with a qualified health practitioner.)

» *Unable to concentrate*

» *Feeling nauseous*

» *Headaches*

» *Dizziness, feeling as though you are walking outside of your physical body*

» *Craving fatty food or something heavy to eat*

» *Tripping over, unbalanced physically*

» *Feeling extremely irritable or stressed*

» *Feeling tired and very physically heavy.*

Quick and easy ways to ground yourself

You can easily ground yourself at home or work by doing any of the following.

Connecting to the earth

By sitting on the ground, letting the sand or dirt run through your fingers and feeling the soft textures automatically re-energises you. Lie down on the grass or walk without your shoes on and feel the earth and grass under your bare feet, walking without shoes on with the soft thick green grass pushing up through your toes. Reconnect with Mother Earth's energy through the soil and ground.

Connecting to the sun

Feeling the sun on your face immediately removes any negativity. How can the dark heavy energy be around you when the sun is so warm and bright? Don't think that the light from fluorescent tubes or halogen lamps can replace sunlight; there is no natural energy in this kind of light.

Connecting to water

Walking through water, whether it is salt water from a sea or water from a lake, river or dam can also give you the most amazing recharge of energy.

What I'm trying to highlight is the difference between the energy in natural settings and naturally occurring things such as wood, grass, water, earth, etc., and manmade things like concrete and plastic. If we surround ourselves with manmade products all the time it removes us from our own inner source of connection with Mother Earth. Plant a garden or just place your hand on a tree trunk and feel the grounding energy come through the bark.

If you look at young children most of them have a natural drive to want to be outside, to get dirty, to roll on the grass, pick up mud, and play with water or feel the sun on their face. Do you remember the joy of seeing ants in the grass, or trying to catch lizards or butterflies? This connection with the natural world seems to leave some people as they grow older and become distracted by the newest mod cons, TV, video games and things that prevent you from enjoying nature.

During our middle years, life can seem monotonous and feel as if we are disconnected from what our true source is. Some people move onto retirement age and realise what they have been missing out on — a connectedness to their life source.

Have you noticed how the elderly usually are drawn to gardening, fishing, planting or lawn bowls? These activities reconnect them with the earth once more; there is a subconscious understanding of the need for connection outside of the material world. The life cycle comes full circle, almost like a remembrance back to the connections to the natural world that they had as a child.

Connecting if you live in the city

You may not have an ocean or mountain near where you live but you can adapt to your own natural surroundings. You may have precious gems near you that you haven't realised are close by. If you live in an inner city suburb full of industrial or commercial buildings and apartments here are a few things that you can do.

> » *Go near a window or balcony that faces the sun or try to get down outside where you can be in the direct sunlight away from the shadow of buildings. Position your face so that you can feel the sunlight on your face, feel its warmth, feel the energy it gives you. Imagine this energy going down from your face all the way through your shoulders, arms to your fingers, back down your chest to your waist. The warmth and energy will flow through to your legs and feet, recharging you.*

> » *If there isn't a park or patch of grass near you, create your own piece of nature. Try to have at least one plant in your home, so that you can touch the leaves and reconnect. I know it sounds airy-fairy but each plant has its own special energy.*

> » *Try to get out of the city when you can, even if it's to a local park to walk or lie on the grass.*

> » *You may like to plant your own garden or vegetable patch.*

> » *You can do everything that has been written above and add to it.*

Look for your own special areas where you live. Is there a local nature reserve or park? Do you have a creek, dam or river that you can access? If you have a courtyard can you have planter boxes on it that you can grow vegetables or plant your favourite flowers?

It's time for us to reconnect with a lot of the old ways. I am not saying that you need to move to acreage and live a life similar to the Amish but, hey, if that is what you want to do that is wonderful too! Try to make changes in your life to see the beauty around you in any of your living situations.

If you do feel like you are missing something or are feeling disconnected or ungrounded, try to reconnect with your surroundings and you will notice a massive difference.

Other ways to connect and to help you ground yourself

Bathing or swimming

A deep, warm bath can be very grounding especially when you add bath salts. If you don't have a bath, you can have a shower and imagine the water is like a beautiful purifying waterfall flowing over your head, shoulders and body.

Swimming or walking in the ocean is also a great way to ground. Salt is naturally grounding and purifying.

Eating grounding foods

The first thing I often do when I have overloaded myself by doing too many psychic readings is to eat heavy foods to ground myself. I usually crave fatty foods such as hot chips — obviously this is not a good thing to always do. There are many other healthy food alternatives that you can eat that will help you to ground your energy. Some of the healthier food options are the old-fashioned foods such as mashed potatoes, porridge, pasta and rice. If the food has been grown in the earth is especially grounding, for example, root vegetables such as potatoes, carrots and onions. Pumpkins and unrefined grains are also very grounding.

In some Western cultures there are a lot of people who are on diets to lose weight and many people tend to cut out certain food groups and do not replace those foods with something else to balance their diets. This can sometimes lead to a feeling of being irritable, light-headed and not being grounded too.

I am not saying that everyone should go out and start eating unhealthy fatty foods or too many carbohydrates, just look at balance in the diet. The old-fashioned foods such as potatoes, pasta, bread and cereals are not only grounding but have a very calming effect on children/adults. If you have carbohydrates for your dinner it can help you to relax and go to sleep.

Walking and exercising

Walk near the trees in your neighbourhood and nearby parks. Walking can be very meditative and can help you to relax. As you walk let all your worries release through the soles of your feet. Breathe in the fresh air around you.

Grounding crystals

You can ground yourself quickly and easily by holding or wearing a crystal to centre yourself and regain your spiritual and emotional balance.

Some of my favourite crystals to use for grounding are:

» *tiger's eye*

» *red jasper*

» *hematite*

» *black obsidian*

» *black tourmaline.*

Grounding sprays/ spritzers/ essential oils and incense

There are many different aromas or sprays that can be used to clear the energy around you and also clear your surroundings. You can spray a spritzer above your head and let the mist fall over your head and shoulders or you can spray it around your environment in your home and workplace. Incense and essential oils can also be burnt to clear energy and ground you.

Grounding meditation and music

Music is an incredibly useful tool in meditation, whether it is listening to relaxation music with floaty piano and nature sounds, or Tibetan chanting, or even Native American flute or drumming music. Each person will be drawn to different music and each sound will resonate differently and have its own energy. Some people may prefer to have complete silence around them when they meditate.

A grounding meditation is different to a relaxation meditation as it shouldn't leave you feeling sleepy; you should feel strong, centred and grounded afterwards. I have included my own grounding meditation exercise for you to try.

GROUNDING MEDITATION EXERCISE

You may want to read this meditation aloud and record it so you can meditate without having to stop and read the instructions. Or you may like to do this meditation with a friend or partner so that you can read it out for each other. After a few times you may not even need to read or hear this meditation.

1 Stand or sit with your feet hip-width apart. Make sure you have room to spread your arms out.

2 Close your eyes and take a deep breath in. As you breathe out let go of any worry or anxiety, let these things float from your mind. Breathe in slowly, then breathe out slowly, breathe in again and breathe out again.

3 When you are ready visualise yourself standing in the middle of a beautiful lush, green forest. Breathe in the cool moist air. Around you are huge trees with big, thick trunks. These trees are so tall that you have to look high into the sky to see the branches and green leaves.

4 Now that you can see the trees all around you, visualise that you are now one of these trees. You are one of the big tall trees in the forest.

5 Your feet and toes feel very heavy as they are like the tree roots, your body is the tree trunk, your arms and hands are branches which spread right up and out towards the warm sun.

6 As you stand tall in the forest visualise your toes turning into tree roots pushing through the floor/ earth deep down through each layer of the earth.

Finally your tree roots reach a big ball of bright white light.

7   Breathe in, breathe out and see the white light travelling up from the tree roots right up through the layers of the earth, up, up and up into your legs which are now like the tree trunk.

8   Breathe in and out again and see the light travel even further up through your stomach, up to your chest, out to your arms and finger tips. The light then travels back through your arms to your neck and up through your head, with the light pouring out the crown of your head.

9   You should now feel very strong, grounded and revitalised. Bring your awareness back to where you are now. Keeping your eyes closed, wiggle your toes and fingers. Stretch your arms up above your head and shake your shoulders. Open your eyes and know that you are now grounded and strong.

If you have your own meditation that you like to use, keep doing what suits you best. This is just one option available and is an example of how easy it is to ground yourself through meditation. It can take time to learn to meditate; don't be too hard on yourself if you find it difficult to focus or visualise things in meditation. Take your time and try to find out what suits you best.

How do you ground yourself?

Answer the questions below to see what you may already be doing consciously or subconsciously to ground your energy.

1. Do you like to walk outside or sit on the grass in the sun?

_____

_____

_____

_____

2. Is there a particular crystal you feel drawn to which may help you to feel protected and grounded? List crystals.

_____

_____

_____

_____

3. Do you like to have a long bath or swim after a long stressful day?

_____

_____

_____

4. Write down anything you currently do to unwind when you are stressed, for example, listen to music, exercise, etc.

_____

_____

_____

5. Is there a particular food that you feel drawn to when you need to ground yourself? Write it down.

_____

_____

_____

_____

6. Think about when your most stressful time of the day or week is, write it down.

_____

_____

_____

_____

7. Now focus on what makes you relax the most and when is the most relaxing time of the day or week for you.

_____

_____

_____

_____

8. Are there any particular people around you that make you feel extremely drained or tired? List them.

_____

_____

_____

_____

_____

9. Is there a certain place or thing that makes you feel uncomfortable or stressed, for example, shopping centres, confined spaces, large crowds? List them.

_____

_____

_____

_____

10. Look at all the questions you have answered and list what you think you need to do to help yourself to become more grounded and balanced in your energy. What can you do to make sure you are feeling confident, energetic and connected with your own sense of self?

_____

_____

_____

_____

_____

_____

_____

_____

_____

_____

_____

_____

_____

Shielding

Shielding is the term used to put an energetic shield or defence up around yourself physically, emotionally or spiritually to protect yourself or others. Usually there are two uses for shields. The first use of the shield is to hide a person visually or energetically so that they aren't noticed. The second way a shield is used is to block any incoming attacks or any unwanted energy.

Shielding is extremely important to keep negativity out of your energy field. Before you begin to undertake any spiritual practice it is important to shield yourself because you are opening yourself up to contact with other people and other spirits who may have positive or negative energy. This protecting technique is not just for people who work in spiritual areas; all people should learn to do this.

There are a few different situations where you may need to shield yourself.

» *When you are talking to someone or are near someone who often complains and is quite negative. Sometimes there are people around you that you may notice are very draining or very energy sapping. You often feel exhausted after they have left you or you just feel like you have been on an emotional rollercoaster.*

» *As some people don't realise that they are being draining you can do things to protect yourself from this. In spiritual circles we sometimes call these types of people 'psychic vamps'. This isn't a very nice term but it does give you an idea of what happens when you are around these people.*

» *When you are doing spiritual work alone or with other people you must shield so that only higher energies come forward. It's important to make sure that you are psychically protected when doing spiritual work so that you work only with the highest positive spiritual vibrations and entities. If you do not know who you are working with you may have a negative or earthbound spirit attach themselves to you or feed you incorrect information.*

» *When you want to keep your family and yourself safe, for example, on trips or holidays, driving in the car or for overall wellbeing.*

» *When you are going into a very busy, draining environment.*

» *When you are feeling anxious or tired and*
need extra energy.

WAYS TO SHIELD YOURSELF

People unconsciously protect their energy by crossing their legs and arms. Have you ever watched someone's body language when they feel insecure or are feeling defensive? Often they will have their arms crossed over their chest, which is a natural defence mechanism. It protects their heart, breast and lung area.

Little children naturally try to put a shield in front of themselves when they are scared. It may be a blanket pulled up over their heads, hiding behind their parents' legs or escaping behind the lounge chair or table. As we all grow older we realise that this does not actually help us and we need to use different methods of shielding, whether it's physical shielding or spiritual shielding.

Many different cultures have used energy shielding as part of their everyday life for protection and spiritual empowerment. Warriors have used physical shields for centuries to block any attacks both up close and from a distance.

In Japan, the ancient samurais would use special rituals or charms to protect their energy. It was a form of invisible, spiritual armour which added extra protection along with the physical armour that protected their body.

Some of the Native American tribes have traditionally used medicine shields that were physical shields made of animal skin stretched over a circular wooden hoop to protect not only themselves and their animals in warfare, but also for spiritual shielding as well. Great care was given to each shield as it was being made.

The warrior would pray over the shield and make sure it was adorned with very personal pictures of his animal totems. Feathers would hang from the bottom of the shield and charms would add to the protective energy of it. Even after the shield was no longer needed for war, it still played a very important part in tribal life. The shield would be hung in a very important place within the lodge or tipi. On a sunny clear day the warrior would even hang his special shield outside the front of his lodging facing towards the east for protection. When the warrior died his shield would be buried with him.

CREATE YOUR OWN PROTECTIVE SPIRIT SHIELD

You may like to create or draw your own protective spirit shield. You don't have to use animal skins; it can just as easily be made with canvas or paper. The important thing is the intent behind it.

1. Go for a walk in nature or sit quietly and focus on what is important for you to put on the spirit shield. (Remember that the spirit shield is to be used for protection for you and your home environment.)

2. Relax, take a deep breath in and out. Ask in your mind for your spirit guides or angels to show you what you most need to help you to stay protected. Pay attention to anything that you see or sense. You may physically see an animal in front of you or in your mind, or a word, colour or symbol. Write down everything that you have seen, felt or experienced.

3. If you have difficulty visualising any symbols or animals try to think about what the most powerful symbols are for you, for example, a bear, wolf, etc.

4. Concentrate on asking for protection and guidance as you draw or make the shield. To make your shield cut out a circular piece of treated animal skin, cloth (muslin), cardboard, paper or canvas.

5. Decorate and paint your material with any of the symbols you have felt or seen. Usually the focus of the shield is a natural symbol or power object such as an animal or weather element. You may like to add beads or bundles of two or three feathers bound together to hang off the shield.

Place your spirit shield in a safe place so you can see it regularly, making it a point of focus for you to help you feel safe and protected.

Remember there is no rush as this process may take many days or even weeks to complete.

LOWER ENTITIES/DRAINING ENERGY

Lower enitities and draining energies can be a cause for stress and a feeling of melancholy, tiredness or discomfort. These energies are unpleasant and the best way to deal with them is to identify them and determine the best way to get rid of this negativity.

There are a number of signs that indicate you may have a lower entity attached to your energy. These signs include:

» *stress and a feeling of melancholy*

» *tiredness or discomfort*

» *depression*

» *headaches*

» *a feeling of not feeling like your normal self*

» *acting erratically.*

There is no need to worry too much if you experience these effects. By becoming more aware of your psychic skills you can have more control of the energies you attract and choose to work only with spirits of the white light or pure energy that consists of love and positivity. Being aware that lower entities exist and can try to drain you or attach themselves to you allows you to psychically protect yourself and keep yourself grounded as much as possible.

Not only do people who are working with their psychic ability experience psychic attack, people who are unaware of the spiritual world can be affected as well. Adults, teenagers and children all experience energy around them and they experience things in different ways.

How does psychic energy affect people?

Children

Children have a very open and pure energy as they have a tendency to be the shining light in the dark. They are so innocent and raw that they do not even know that they are sometimes susceptible to psychic attack or draining negative energy.

The way that children experience negative energy can happen in different ways. It can manifest in the form of nightmares, fear of being alone in the dark, fear of sleeping, anxiety around big groups of people, stomach aches, headaches and fear of death or dying.

Often children will also be able to feel negative energy in and around people they come in contact with. Children are very intuitive and go on their gut instincts about people. Have you ever noticed a baby or young child cry or flat out refuse to go to a particular person? Sometimes this is purely because the child is shy or scared of strangers but other times there may be a particular energy about that person that the child is picking up on.

Teenagers

Teenagers are a tricky bunch as they are not as open and pure as younger children and are not as shut off as some adults. Teenagers tend to have energies which spike up and down very dramatically due to hormones and changes in their life experiences.

If a teenager is quite open psychically they can absorb their friends, family members and other people's energies both positive and negative. When a hormonal teenager is feeling quite depressed it can be any number of things that are going on around them, but one of the things that many people don't realise is that they may be carrying other people's energy which is draining them or making them depressed.

The way that a teen can be carrying energy other than their own is through being an empathetic; they can feel other people's pain, or emotions. They may not realise it but they may think it is them that feels sick or depressed, but it could be that they have been around someone else that feels that way.

Another thing that is commonly seen are teenagers becoming interested in their own psychic abilities or searching for something exciting and new to do. Often they decide to try to play with an Ouija board to call on ghosts or spirits like they have seen on TV shows or scary movies. This is meant to be purely just a game of fun but they do not know what they are dealing with.

The Ouija board is an incredibly dangerous tool to be used if the people using it do not know what they are doing. The reason it's dangerous is the people who mess around with the Ouija are not psychically protecting themselves and do not know who or what they are letting in spiritually. They open a gate to the spirit world and lower entities/negative energies are able to enter and attach themselves to the people who are around the Ouija board.

This can make the teens feel angry, aggressive, depressed, suicidal, manic, and even hear voices which are not their spirit guides. When this happens it can be due to other factors such as mental issues, depression, etc. but it can also be due to a negative spirit attaching itself to the teenager.

Adults
Just as the children and teens can experience negative energy adults can too. If adults are open psychically and

do not engage in proper psychic activity they are also susceptible to the same things we have listed with the teens.

PROTECTION FOR YOURSELF, YOUR FAMILY AND YOUR HOME

By clearing your environment and yourself regularly you can continue to be happy and move forward in your life. There are various ways to psychically protect yourself and your environment.

Smudging

Smudging is a traditional ceremony which involves using specific herbs which are lit with fire to create a protective smoke around a person, object or a place. This process is used to banish any negative entities or energies.

The word smudging comes from the Native American culture but there are many different indigenous cultures which have their own type of ritual or smudging which focuses on bringing balance back to the environment, the place or to the person physically, spiritually and mentally.

Many religious practices from all different cultures also smudge without calling it smudging, for example, in the Catholic Church priests use incense with frankincense in it for religious ceremonies and to purify and protect the church and its clergy. It is also said that ancient samurais as far back as the 14th century would waft incense smoke over their armour and helmets for protection and purification.

To create a sacred place to live in or work from it's important that you have smudged the area and have a positive intent which you embed into that area. I like to use a few different techniques to make an area protected. Smudging is done with smudge sticks, spritzers with essential oils or incense. The first thing I do when I move into a new home or work space is smudge the area.

 ## How to smudge your home or work environment

To smudge a home or workplace it is best that the room is quite dark and that you will not be interrupted. The herbs traditionally used are cedar, sweet grass and sage. The herbs can be bound together with twine to form a stick or they can be placed in a shell (the traditional shell is an abalone or paua shell, also known as the ormer shell in the United Kingdom), or a clay or stone bowl which is heat resistant or has sand or soil in it to prevent it from overheating.

Many traditional Native American elders prefer people to use clay or stone bowls instead of the abalone shells so as not to misuse the abalone shell energy. They feel it should be used for use with water, not to be misused or burnt by fire.

Sage can be used by itself in a smudge stick and it's traditionally used to get rid of bad energy or spirits, and to keep any negativity from entering a place. It can also be broken up and placed in a bowl and lit with cedar and sweet grass.

Cedar is burnt like sage, in a bowl to carry prayers up to the Universe and to purify an area.

Sweet grass is a very sacred herb that is used to welcome and bring in good spirits and energy. Sweet grass is sometimes hard to come by, especially in Australia, but it is well worth trying to find it. You will find sweet grass usually sold in long plaited braids. If you use these sweet grass plaits you can light the end of the plait and use the smoke to smudge, the same way you do with the sage. You can also shave parts of the sweet grass off and burn it in a bowl with the cedar and sage.

Just as the herbs are important the intent with which you smudge is just as important. It is very important that you smudge when you are ready to clear out any old, negative, stale energy and you feel that you are focused.

When smudging your home or work environment start in the most northern part of your home or work. Walk with the smudge stick lit and smoking in a clockwise direction starting at the north. Fan the smoke around each corner of your home and ask for all negativity to be removed. Imagine the area filled with bright white light. As you walk around in a clockwise direction you should end up back at your original starting point. This is important so that it completes the purification process.

 ## SMUDGING YOURSELF

The intent behind the smudging is just as important as the actual smudging herbs themselves. Fan the smoke over your body and face with the use of a feather (you can use a special large feather or if you don't have a feather just use your hands), to purify yourself.

You can smudge yourself with just one of the above herbs or you can make it a three-step process.

1 Start with sage to clear out the negative energy.

2 Move onto cedar to purify yourself.

3 Finish with sweet grass to bring in positive energy.

Once you have smudged yourself or your environment it's important that you open all windows and let the negativity out. Do not blow the smudge stick out, snuff it out in the bowl or into the earth.

Note: It's important that you do not smudge in closed areas if you are pregnant, have babies or small children around, or are asthmatic. You may like to use an incense stick or a spritzer spray instead as they are just as powerful. Remember that the key element of smudging is the intent.

Crystals and creating a protection grid

I also use crystals to create a protection grid in my home, office or anywhere that I am working or teaching. It is a simple process of using four individual amethyst crystal points. Amethyst is a very protective crystal that is great for creating spiritual boundaries and for keeping negative energy out. Crystals used for psychic protection are usually the darker coloured crystals such as amethyst, black onyx, black tourmaline and garnet.

To grid a home or workplace it's important that you smudge the area first and then place one amethyst crystal in each corner of the room (if the room is not a square shape that's ok, make a square as best you can). If you don't have amethyst points or crystals in the shape of a triangle it's ok to use whatever you have. If you do have amethyst points, point the raw end of the crystal inwards to the centre of the imagined square and the darker end outwards to each corner.

Note: If you have small children or pets that may swallow the crystals you may have to place them up high out of harm's way.

You can place the four crystals in each room or just in the four approximate corners of the whole home. I have even placed an amethyst crystal on each of the four corners of my property outside. I bury the crystals in the same way as I place them inside, with the point facing out from the property.

Colours and light

Another thing that I like to do to energetically protect my home or work environment is to visualise golden or white beams of light stretching over my whole property or yard, including from corner to corner, in large sweeping arches. Each arch joins up and glows brightly.

Colours are also another way to shield your energy and extremely important because they affect how we feel and how we come across to other people. White and blue are the traditional colours associated with spiritual protection. In New Mexico in the United States, it is the tradition of the Pueblo Native American tribe to paint their doors, doorframes and windows blue to ward off any evil energy and to protect the house. They believe that blue is a protective colour, as do many of the Arabic countries who use blue to ward off the evil eye or negative energy.

I find it interesting that blue has been such a protective colour for so many different types of cultures. I remember back eleven years ago when my husband and I bought our first home, the home we are still living in. The first thing I felt drawn to do was paint the front door, front steps and all of the outdoor window sills a deep dark blue. Back then I didn't even know about the tradition of the Pueblo tribe or any other culture relating to the colour blue. I just intuitively felt it should be that colour.

As I sit here writing, I am sitting in my new studio that has just finished being built and guess what? The colours of the external walls are the same deep dark blue. I think it may be a colour that my spirit guides like me to live and work around.

When I am doing my mediumship shows or events I will usually wear a darker pair of tights or pants to help ground me and protect me and a lighter top to lighten up the energy so it's not so heavy.

Psychic protection using white light

I affirm to the Universe and ask in my mind for my property or anything that I want protected to be protected by the white light and for no negativity to enter.

Talismans

Just as colours are important to wear, so are some pieces of jewellery or talismans. I wear a silver ring with a big oval black onyx crystal twenty-four hours a day to protect my energy due to the high volume of people I see and sense in my everyday life. Not only does the crystal protect my energy it is also a visual reminder to me. Every time I look down at my hand and see it I remember to get rid of excess energy to shield and ground when I can.

To other people who see me I must look a bit odd I have to say, because not only do I have my black onyx ring, I also have my piece of striped red, yellow, black and white cotton string that is wound around my left wrist three times and tied. This is a special piece of cotton because of the intent behind it. It was blessed by my Tibetan Buddhist monk friend Lama Tendar. I regularly travel with the mind body and spirit festivals throughout Australia appearing onstage. Tendar travels to the same festivals and I often go to him for his amazing healings. After my most recent healing a few months ago, Tendar tied a piece of cotton string around my left wrist. He blessed it and told me it was for protection. I was not to take it off but if it fell off that was ok; I was to then throw it out. This piece of string is still on my wrist, who knows how long it will take to fall off or deteriorate. (I was talking to another person who we travel with who runs the stage; he told me his protection string lasted two years.)

You can use anything as a protection tool or talisman as long as you believe in it and you make it so. My simple piece of cotton has so much power for me because of who blessed it and because of my deep belief system in what it represents.

Positive affirmations

By asserting yourself and positively affirming to the Universe that you are protected you will be able to stay strong psychically and strengthen your energy. You can choose whatever affirmation you like and whatever feels right for you. I like to use the following affirmations when I feel the need to strengthen my energy shields.

> » *My family and I are filled with love and light and are protected from all negativity.*

> » *I surround myself with white light and only the positive energy of the Universe may enter my personal space.*

Visualisations

Another way to shield is by visualising yourself protected inside of something such as a bubble of light or anything that you feel drawn to that you feel protected in. It can be hard at first to visualise the bubble so you may like to draw a picture of a circle with a person inside of it. Focus on the drawing and use that image as a reference point when you need to shield your energy.

THE BUBBLE OF LIGHT VISUALISATION

The bubble of light visualisation can be used on a regular basis whenever you feel it is necessary, or you may like to use it as well as another type of shielding exercise. You can mix and match a few of the different shielding techniques when you feel like you need a change or extra protection.

1. Imagine a bubble of bright light in front of you. You can choose what colour the bubble is. I like to use pink or purple because it doesn't shine so brightly as the white. It still is protective but it has a more muted colour which adds to the protection.

2. See the bubble floating in front of you, visualise that it has a big zip running down the front of it. This

bubble is so strong and protective that nothing can penetrate it.

3 When you are ready, try to imagine yourself unzipping the zip and see yourself climbing inside of the bubble. Once you are inside the bubble turn around and zip the zip back up to the top of the bubble.

4 You can now think and affirm that you are now completely safe and protected. Nothing can harm you.

You can also use this exercise to place other people such as your friends, kids, partners, pets and family in their own protective energy bubble.

The cloak, the sword and the castle visualisation

Often when I teach shielding some of my students prefer to use a different method to shield themselves. They like to visualise a protective cloak wrapped around them, or a tall brick castle which shields them and protects them.

With the protective cloak as a shield, I had a student who would imagine a whole cupboard full of long dark cloaks. Each cloak would look the same on the outside, but on the inside would be a different bright coloured satin lining.

When this student felt she needed extra protection she would go for the colour that she related to strength, such as red, or if she needed to connect with spirit and wanted to be protected yet relaxed she would pick a light blue. Each colour had a meaning and purpose which was special to her. This may suit you or you may like to try something a bit different.

Other people I have met imagine a strong silver sword in front of them gleaming with bright white light, stopping anything from entering their energy space. I have also heard of people imagining mirrors placed all around them, so if anything comes near them that is negative it is reflected straight back and not absorbed by their energy.

These visualisations may sound very sci-fi or imaginative but they are very effective. You have to remember that the important thing about psychic protection is your intent behind it. If you are feeling strong, in control and asserting your right to be protected, it will happen.

Note: When you are first learning it's important to use a shielding method that is quick and easy for you to remember. Don't be scared or become too obsessed with psychic protection, just think of it as a kind of sunscreen that protects your skin. Shielding is protecting your spiritual skin.

Lower entities

I have experienced some encounters with lower entities in my life that sometimes make me feel scared even though I am a professional psychic medium and have had this gift since I was a young girl. I am not trying to scare you but I do feel it's helpful to explain things to you in a truthful way based on my own personal experiences.

The times that stand out to me the most are the times of feeling a lower entity or negative spirit physically trying to gain energy from me. Throughout the years I have had a few experiences where I have been asleep, healthy and happy, minding my own business, until I've woken up panicking and not being able to breathe. I gasp for breath and it feels as if I have something heavy on my chest trying to draw the breath out of me.

Some people may instantly think that I had a cold or chest infection that can make you feel like that, or perhaps an asthma attack. Let me tell you that there have been times when I have obviously had that happen when I have been sick with the flu or a cold, but the times I am talking about are the times when I am completely healthy.

When this happens I am awake but it is as though I cannot use my voice or call out. I have a feeling of being helpless and unable to breathe. It feels as though a negative energy is all around me and it can be very scary.

Each time this happens I have to stop myself from panicking and think quickly about what to do to get rid of the energy. In this instance I use my mind. I try to calm myself down to relax my breathing. Once I relax myself a bit I feel stronger and more able to demand the energy be removed. I focus all my mental energy on demanding in my strongest thought form that the negativity to be removed immediately. I demand this three times.

After asserting myself I then call upon Archangel Michael, who is a very strong protective energy, to come and remove the negativity from around me. Within seconds I feel the energy pull back and I breathe easily again. This whole process seems like it is going on for hours but in reality it may be only a few seconds or minutes.

I am not the only person to experience this. Over the years I have spoken to many of my students, friends and family members who have experienced similar events. They just haven't been able to verbalise what it was or haven't understood what was happening.

You may be thinking how does this happen and why does this happen if you are already psychically protected? I was thinking the same thing and asked my spirit guides about it as well. The answer they gave me was that even if you do psychically protect yourself sometimes there are some lower entities or energies that can get through, like the odd stray tea leaf that may find it's way into your tea cup through the tea bag. It's annoying but you can easily remove it.

The second reason they gave me was that it reminds me to psychically protect myself. Sometimes I am blasé about things and just expect everything to be all right. When something like this happens it reminds me to pay more attention to the spirit world and to be careful with what I am doing psychically.

Now please don't go and think that this is definitely going to happen to you. You may never experience this. I work with the spirit world every single day which means it is bound to happen to me more regularly. You may just get the heebie jeebies every now and again and feel as if something is not right or something or someone is watching you. That may be the way you experience the energy of a lower entity.

PART
Two

Psychic tools

Tools and techniques to heighten your intuition

PENDULUMS

A pendulum is used for accessing information which our normal senses cannot access. It helps us to tap into our Higher Self and enhances our intuition. Divining with a pendulum has been around for many centuries and is an ancient spiritual art form. Pendulums can be used for various things such as finding missing objects and missing people, locating water, minerals and oil, but what we are concentrating on here is using the pendulum for divination (connecting with spirit to help us answer questions we need to know about).

To make a pendulum you can use any everyday item such as a ring, a coin, a pendant or a key. Choose whatever feels right for you to use. It's important that the shape is symmetrical and has a point. Once you have chosen your item, making sure it is not too heavy or too light, you can suspend it from a piece of string that is about 15 to 20 centimetres long or a necklace.

Pendulum exercises

 HOW TO USE A PENDULUM

Ground yourself and ask for protection from your spirit guides. As you sit down relax and get comfortable. Try to relax your mind.

If you would like to sit at a table you can rest your elbow on the table in front of you or you can rest your elbow on your knee. Whatever way you choose make sure your hand is steady and allow the pendulum to swing freely back and forth.

When you are ready to begin using your pendulum think the following statement in your mind.

'I, (your name), the owner of this pendulum, declare that only those of the white light can respond to my questions when using this pendulum; I promise to use my pendulum only for good.'

Please remember that using your pendulum is not a game — it's a serious form of communication with your spirit guide. Always check that the spirits you are talking with through your pendulum are from the light.

When you first use your pendulum you need to find out which way your pendulum swings for you for your 'yes' and 'no' answers. It can take time but this will allow you to have a clear answer swing to your pendulum.

It is always good to ask practice questions first when you are using your pendulum just to make sure that you are sure that you are getting the right information. I like to start by asking if I am female.

This is an easy question and the pendulum should swing in the direction of my 'yes' which is forwards and backwards. The second question I then ask is if I am male, another obvious question and the pendulum should swing side to side for my 'no' answer because I am female.

My pendulum sometimes swings around and around in circles when I am not meant to know what the answer is or if I have asked the same question too many times. This is my spirit guide's way of saying 'enough is enough' we have already answered you or they are telling me that I'm not meant to know the answer to that question.

When I am confident that my pendulum is working correctly with my energy I begin asking very specific questions that I would like answers to. Always make sure your questions have a specific 'yes' or 'no' answer for this to work, for example, 'Is Sam going to get the job he applied for today at the cd store?' If you were to ask a question that was too open-ended it will be hard for you to get a correct answer, for example, ' Will Sam ever pull his socks up and work anywhere?' You may get an answer of yes or no but you won't know the specifics of where the job will be or when he will get it unless you ask.

CHAKRAS

There are seven main chakra points (energy centres) found in the human body. These chakra points are responsible for the energy flow between our spiritual and physical bodies.

Chakras are found in the aura and they run from the crown of the head to the base of the spine. They also run across the body horizontally. People who can see chakras often describe them as spinning wheels of light.

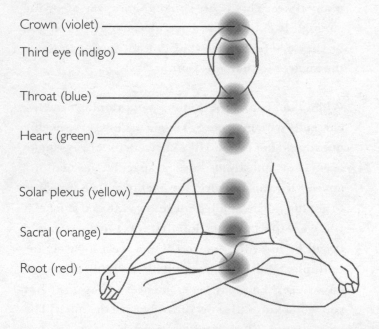

Crown (violet)

Third eye (indigo)

Throat (blue)

Heart (green)

Solar plexus (yellow)

Sacral (orange)

Root (red)

How chakras affect us

Sometimes our chakra energy can become blocked. When a chakra is blocked or disrupted it can make the person feel ill, depressed or tired. If a chakra is running clearly and properly a person can feel energetic, uplifted, positive and healthy. I feel it's important to look closely at each chakra so that you can see how each chakra feels when it is closed and underactive, overactive or open and running properly.

Chakra	Open/ running properly
Root or base — grounding	You will feel grounded, open, confident, stable and secure.
Sacral — sexuality and passion	You can express yourself well. You are passionate, energetic and enjoy intimacy and you are comfortable with your own sexuality.
Solar plexus — personal and emotional power	You feel as if you are in control of your own personal power, you can assert yourself and make decisions for yourself. You have good self-esteem and confidence in yourself.
Heart — relationships and love	You will be compassionate, very loving and considerate to others around you. You feel like you can express yourself in a loving way and can help others. You like to be in a harmonious environment. You give love and receive love in relationships.

Closed/underactive	Overactive
You may feel tense, nervous, insecure and frightened easily.	You may resist change and become stagnant. You may become materialistic and begin to focus only on your own needs.
You may have emotional walls up and find it hard to express yourself. You may find it hard to let people in and be passionate and intimate with others.	You may find yourself becoming too emotional. You tend to attach yourself to people quite quickly and you tend to have a high sex drive or be very sexual with others. Relationships are very important to you.
You may feel insecure and unable to make decisions for yourself. You may not like to express your needs in a group environment and would rather go with the flow then cause conflict. You may sometimes be submissive or shy in expressing your needs to others.	You may feel as if your way is the only way, you may not listen to other people's opinions or ideas. You may be aggressive and very controlling. You may like to dominate others and may have problems with self-control issues.
You are unable to express yourself in a loving way to others. You may feel like you are blocked and unable to handle a relationship. You may not want to let other people see your emotions.	You can sometimes be too emotionally attached to other people. You may constantly need to express your love and be loved; this may make people feel smothered by your love and energy. You may be in love with the idea of being in love and you may be in a relationship for selfish, self-serving reasons.

Chakra	Open/ running properly
Throat — expression and communication	You will have no problems with communicating and expressing what you need to say. You are confident in a group environment. You may also be able to confidently express yourself easily in a creative manner such as: singing, writing, acting or art.
Third eye — intuition	You will be open to the Universe and spiritual ideas and concepts. You are intuitive. You think outside the box and realise that there are many different ways of life. You tend to listen to your own inner knowledge.
Crown — higher knowledge	You will be aware of your own inner knowledge. You will be very sensitive to your needs and the needs of others. You will be very open to people of all kinds of races, sex and personality types. You will feel very comfortable with who you are and what your role is in this world in this life.

Closed/underactive	Overactive
You may be quiet and shy and feel as if you cannot speak or express yourself. You may feel anxious in front of large groups of people and try to keep your ideas to yourself.	You may be domineering and tend to talk too much. Sometimes you may not listen to other people and you may tend to push people away by being too loud and argumentative.
You may not be able to think outside the box, you may have a closed-minded approach to things. You may rely on others to make decisions for you and you may feel as if you need to follow a set of rigid instructions.	You may not be grounded in reality; you may be walking with your head in the clouds and fantasising too much. You may be too focused on the spiritual world and not focusing on the practical things in life.
You may be quite judgmental or you might have a closed mind. You may feel as if there is no point in spirituality and intuition.	You may be obsessed with your spiritual needs and spirituality. You will not be grounded and you may tend to force your spirituality onto other people. You may be thinking too much and not paying attention to the practical needs of yourself and others.

How do you think your chakras are running?

Now that you've read about the different effects you will experience emotionally and physically with the way that your chakras are running, I would like you to do a quick exercise to see what you feel about each of your seven chakras.

Do you think that each chakra is open and running properly, closed, underactive or overactive? It's important that you are honest with yourself so that you can get the most benefit out of this exercise.

 FOCUSING ON YOUR CHAKRAS

Take time to quieten your mind, close your eyes and begin to focus on each chakra in your body, starting with your base chakra. Go through each of your chakras and write down if you think they are currently open and running properly, closed, underactive or overactive.

Also take time to write down why you think your chakra is running the way it is, for example, if you feel that your heart chakra is underactive or closed, is it because you have been hurt in your relationship area and you are still carrying the residual energy?

Base chakra (located at the base of your spine)

_____

_____

_____

Sacral chakra (located near your navel and sexual organs)

_____

_____

_____

Solar plexus chakra (located below your breastbone above your navel)

_____

_____

_____

Heart chakra (located in the middle of your chest to the middle of your shoulderblades)

_____

_____

_____

Throat chakra (located in the throat area)

_____

_____

_____

Third eye chakra (located between your eyebrows in the centre of your forehead)

_____

_____

_____

Crown chakra (located at the top of your head on the crown of your head)

_____

_____

_____

Please don't worry or panic if you realise that some of your chakras are not running in the way that you want them to, there are some very quick and easy techniques that I will show you to help open up your chakras.

Chakra crystals — specific crystals for each chakra

Crystals can be used to realign the body's natural energy vibration and to balance out the chakras. Each chakra has a colour and crystals are used that match the colour of the chakra.

First base chakra — snowflake obsidian (dark colours)

Snowflake obsidian is a very powerful crystal. It also helps with the following things:

» *grounding, psychic protection*

» *cuts through negative thought patterns*

» *shows you where your truth is*

» *balances male/female energies*

Physically snowflake obsidian helps with:

» *clearing the eyes*

» *smoothing the skin*

» *treatment of veins.*

Additional crystals for the base chakra

Hematite is a crystal that helps to ground and remove negative energies. It helps you to feel more self-confident and aids concentration.

Physically, hematite helps with:

» *anxiety*

» *insomnia*

» *blood circulation*

» *headaches*

» *vertigo*

» *removes heat from the body.*

Smoky quartz is a wonderful crystal for grounding during meditation or spirit work. It still lets you reach high vibrations without becoming distracted. It is a very protective crystal which helps you to remove any past hurts and move forward in your life.

Physically, smoky quartz helps with:

» *pain relief*

» *headaches*

» *cramps*

» *reproductive system.*

Second sacral chakra — orange carnelian (orange to red)

Orange carnelian is well known for its ability to enhance a person's vitality, creativity and passion. Carnelian is a very vibrant and protective crystal which helps with the following things:

» *motivation*

» *enhances creativity*

» *promotes positive energy and confidence in oneself*

» *abuse recovery*

» *concentration*

Physically, orange carnelian helps with:

» *fertility and sexual and reproductive organs*

» *depression*

» *arthritis*

» *absorption of vitamins and minerals*

» *metabolism.*

Additional crystals for the sacral chakra

Red jasper is a very grounding crystal. It is protective and helps to align the chakras.

Physically, red jasper helps with:

» *digestive system*

» *blood cleansing*

» *liver*

» *sexual organs*

» *enhances circulation.*

Tangerine quartz is a crystal that balances the sacral chakra and allows your true creativity to come out; it also helps with balancing emotions.

Physically, tangerine quartz helps with:

» *gall bladder*

» *balances kidney, bladder, spleen*

» *reproductive system.*

Third solar plexus chakra- citrine (burnt amber to pale yellow)

Citrine is well known for its ability to bring wealth and abundance; it is usually placed in a wallet/purse or in the wealth corner of a home. Citirine is one of the very few crystals that does not hold any negativity and does not need to be cleansed.

Citrine's bright, creative energy is used for the following things:

» *brings joyful, warm and happy energy, encourages positivity*

» *stimulates creativity and passion*

» *it is very nurturing and helps caregivers and healers*

» *helps manifest dreams and goals*

» *helps with problem solving.*

Physically, citrine helps with:

» *the colon*

» *detoxifies your body*

» *thymus gland*

» *digestive system*

» *bulimia/anorexia.*

Additional crystals for the solar plexus chakra

Tiger eye gold is fantastic to help you ground your energy and feel more stable in your life. It helps you to organise yourself and feel confident in times of change.

Physically tiger eye gold helps with:

» *eyes*

» *the throat*

» *reproductive system*

» *mending broken bones.*

Malachite assists you to change situations when needed, and helps you to release negative emotions and to accept responsibility for your actions.

Physically, malachite helps with:

» *liver*

» *motion sickness*

» *asthma*

» *arthritis.*

Fourth heart chakra — rose quartz (pale pink)

Rose quartz is very well known as a healing crystal for love and relationships; it has a soft nurturing energy encouraging unconditional love in relationships.

Rose quartz is used for the following things:

» *promotes a feeling of peace and self-fulfilment*

» *balances emotions*

» *releases past hurts and makes way for new
relationships*

» *helps you to nurture yourself and others*

» *assists with abuse recovery.*

Physically, rose quartz helps with:

» *period pain*

» *burns*

» *diabetes*

» *fertility*

» *circulation*

» *muscular pain*

Additional crystals for the heart chakra

Jade helps you to feel self-confident, calm and emotionally
balanced. It also helps you with luck and promotes longevity.

Physically, jade helps with:

» *heart*

» *immune system*

- » *asthma*

- » *kidneys*

- » *stimulates hair growth.*

Rhodonite calms and balances out anxiousness. It helps you to heal with love and to gain self-confidence.

Physically, rhodonite helps with:

- » *skeletal system*

- » *immune system*

- » *heart*

- » *throat*

- » *emphysema*

Fifth throat chakra — blue lace agate (pale blue and white)

Blue lace agate is a very soothing and healing crystal that helps you to stay well balanced.

Blue lace agate is used for the following things:

- » *helps you to communicate and voice your opinions*

» *helps you to obtain inner peace and tranquillity*

» *enhances your confidence*

» *encourages you to be patient.*

Physically, blue lace agate helps with:

» *throat, larynx*

» *viruses and fevers*

» *the nervous system*

» *thyroid deficiencies*

» *the neck and shoulders.*

Additional crystals for the throat chakra

Turquoise enhances communication skills, increases intuition and helps form a calm, protective shield around your energy.

Physically, turquoise helps with:

» *headaches*

» *eyes*

» *heart*

» *throat*

» *emotional balance.*

Amazonite helps you to see both sides of problems so you can have an open mind to different perspectives. It is a crystal that balances the male and female energies.

Physically, amazonite helps with:

» *nervous system*

» *throat*

» *heart*

» *muscles*

Sixth third eye chakra — Amethyst (deep purple to light lavender)

Amethyst is a very protective crystal. It is very popular and is one of the most commonly known crystals.

Amethyst is used for the following things:

» *psychic protection and protection of homes*

» *cleanses crystals*

» *helps break bad habits*

» *enhances intuition and psychic ability*

» *helps with nightmares and insomnia, encourages sleep*

» *helps and protects a person during astral travel*

» *absorbs radiation and is great near TVs, microwaves and computers.*

Physically, amethyst helps with:

» *stimulating tissue growth*

» *boosts the immune system*

» *helps eyesight*

» *cleans the blood*

Additional crystals for the third eye chakra

Sodalite helps you to connect with your spirit guides. Sodalite promotes truthful communication and it releases fear and anxieties.

Physically sodalite helps with:

» *thyroid*

» *pancreas*

» *throat*

» *nervous stomach.*

Angelite connects you with higher spiritual beings such as angels and spirit guides. Angelite's soft feathery energy increases your intuition and helps you to remain calm during times of stress.

Physically, angelite helps with:

» *throat*

» *heart*

» *sunburn*

» *stomach ulcer.*

Seventh crown chakra — clear quartz (clear to white)

The Clear quartz crystal is one of the most versatile crystals. It is used for the following things:

» *helps to strengthen the third eye and crown chakras*

» *enhances psychic ability and visions*

» *great for meditation*

» *it can be programmed easily, for example, to be used as a general healing crystal, a reading crystal, etc.*

» *it can help you to access information and help you to find the right answers for decision making.*

Physically cear quartz helps with:

» *the digestive system*

» *vertigo (being afraid of heights) and air travel*

» *burns*

» *re-aligning the chakras.*

Additional crystals for the crown chakra

Fluorite increases your intuition and spiritual understanding and it also clears away negative energy and balances out your chakras. Fluorite calms and centres your energy.

Physically, fluorite helps with:

» *teeth*

» *bones*

» *throat*

» *memory and concentration.*

Apophyllite connects you with your intuition, helps you to find your own sense of inner happiness and it calms your mind.

Physically, apophyllite helps with:

» *yes*

» *throat*

» *memory and concentration.*

A really quick and effective way to balance out your chakras is by using crystals. By using a crystal that is the same colour as the chakra you are working on, you can clear blockages and re-energise your chakras. Use the 'How do you think your chakras are running' exercise on page 76.

Chakra exercises

 FOCUSING ON YOUR CHAKRAS

What you will need:

● **A pendulum**

● **A partner to do the exercise with**

● **A crystal chakra pack with one crystal for each chakra, for example a blue crystal for the throat chakra and so on (see the crystals list on pages 78–92).**

● **Incense stick or smudge stick for clearing the crystals**

● **A pen**

The easiest way to clear all of your chakras at once is to lay down flat on your back and placing the right coloured crystal on each of the corresponding chakra points on your body. You can do this by yourself or it can be easier if you have someone to help you.

When doing a chakra clearing with crystals I always like to work with another person who holds a pendulum over the body. A pendulum is great for identifying which chakras are out in a person's body. (See p.64 on how to make your own pendulum.)

When using a pendulum over a person, get the person to lie on the ground and close their eyes. Ask for your spirit guides to come forward to protect you and your partner and to help you while you are clearing your partner's chakras.

Hold the pendulum approximately five to ten centimetres above the person's body at each of the chakra points. I like to begin at the base chakra first and make my way up to the crown chakra. When trying to see if the person's chakras are balanced you need to focus on how the pendulum is moving or swinging. Usually if the pendulum is spinning clockwise the chakra is running properly and if it is spinning anti-clockwise it may be blocked or running a little bit more slowly.

You can feel the energy in the pendulum as you hold it above the other person's chakra points. If the person lying down has a clear chakra the pendulum should swing around in very strong clockwise circles. The stronger the reaction of the pendulum the clearer the chakra is.

Sometimes the pendulum will not swing at all over the person's chakra points or it will swing from side to side and then stop. This shows you, that chakra may need work or be in need of more balance.

Take note of which chakras need more work and which ones are running smoothly and also write down how strong the pendulum's reaction is.

Base chakra

_____

_____

_____

Sacral chakra

_____

_____

_____

Solar plexus chakra

_____

_____

_____

Heart chakra

_____

_____

_____

Throat chakra

_____

_____

_____

Third eye chakra

_____

_____

_____

Crown chakra

_____

_____

_____

When I teach workshops and do this exercise I often get the students to do this exercise on each other. It's amazing to watch the students and to see which chakras need work and which ones don't. For example, often a very outgoing student, who is quite loud and demonstrative, may have a very open throat chakra which represents their communication skills, but when their base chakra is investigated it can often be out of whack and unbalanced because they are not grounded enough.

Each person relates to the world in different ways so each person has different needs and things that they need to balance in themselves and their lives. Now that you are aware of which chakras need to be balanced you can begin to do a chakra balance using crystals.

CRYSTAL CHAKRA BALANCING

In the same way you worked with a partner and pendulum to find out if your chakras are open or closed, have your partner lie on the floor. Take turns to balance each other out.

Cleanse your crystals. It's very important that you cleanse the crystals each time before you use them to clear the chakras. Crystals can hold energy so you want them to feel clear before you begin the exercise. Remember to cleanse the crystals after you swap with your partner.

After cleansing the crystals, take your incense or smudge stick and light it with a match until it is smoking. Hold the crystals in your hand. Wave the incense or smudge stick around in a clockwise circle three times over the crystals. In your mind ask for all negativity to be removed.

After you have cleansed your crystals select the first crystal for the base chakra. It should be a black, red or brown crystal. As you hold the crystal move your hand in a clockwise direction. Place the crystal on your partner's base chakra which is at the base of the spine. (Note: Your partner will be lying on their back so you can place it on the front of their body resting on their thigh.)

Repeat this exercise for each crystal and chakra point:

- second chakra on the side of the genital area (you can place it on the lower stomach)
- third chakra on the middle stomach area near the navel
- fourth chakra on the heart/chest area
- fifth chakra on the throat
- sixth chakra on the forehead above the eyebrows
- seventh chakra on the crown of the head (you can rest the crystal on the floor next to the crown of the head).

Once you have placed the crystals on each chakra of your partner it's important to let them breathe easily and to feel relaxed for a few minutes. The crystals may start to heat up on the body as they begin to work. Ask your partner if they are feeling any heat or sensations and for which chakra.

After a few minutes it's time to take the crystals off, one at a time, from each chakra of your partner. When you are removing the crystals start at the base chakra and remove the crystal in an anti-clockwise direction. Go through each chakra and remove them in the same way in an anti-clockwise direction.

When you have collected all of the crystals it's time to check if the chakras have all been realigned.

Your partner will need to stay lying down, pick up the pendulum and repeat the process of checking the chakras. Hold the pendulum over each chakra and take note of how each chakra is running after using the crystals.

My students are usually so surprised when they see the dramatic difference in the chakras after using the crystals. It's amazing to see how open the chakras are by using the pendulum.

When you are ready you can swap with your partner and let them clear your chakras.

  CHAKRA BALANCING MEDITATION

During this chakra balancing meditation, see yourself surrounded by a bubble of white light. Know that you are protected at all times. Close your eyes and take a deep breath in, as you breathe out let go of any worries or anxieties. Try to let these things float from your mind

● Breathe in slowly, exhale slowly, breathe in, exhale slowly. Start to feel your body relaxing.

● It is a comfortable feeling. If you are sitting on a chair, your back is supported.

● Your feet are touching the floor. Your arms are relaxed on your lap.

● If you are lying on the floor you are supported by the floor.

● Feel your back relaxing, Your arms and legs are feeling lighter and lighter.

Your head is relaxed. Turn your attention to your base chakra, which is located at the base of your spine. Your base chakra resonates with the colour red. Visualise a red light that is quickly spinning clockwise.

Take a deep breath in, breathe out and focus on your sacral chakra. This chakra is located near your sexual organs. See it as a round orange light spinning clockwise like a wheel. Focus on the orange colour.

Breathe in and breathe out. Move your focus up to your solar plexus chakra that is located near your navel or solar plexus. See it as a round yellow light spinning like a wheel. Focus on the colour yellow.

Now focus on the heart chakra which is located near your chest or heart area. Envision a round green light spinning like a wheel. Focus on the colour green.

Breathe in and breathe out. Move your focus to the throat chakra which is located in your throat area. See it as a round blue light spinning like a wheel. Focus on the colour blue.

You are now nearly all clear with your chakras running very quickly. There are only two more chakras to focus on.

The next chakra for you to focus on is your third eye chakra which is located just above your eyebrows in the centre of your forehead. See it as a round purple light spinning clockwise like a wheel. Focus on the colour purple.

Breathe in and breathe out. Remain relaxed. Finally move your focus to the crown chakra at the top of your head. See it is a round white light spinning like a wheel. Focus on the colour white.

Take a few moments now to relax, you have just opened up, cleared and balanced all of your seven chakras. All seven of your chakras are now spinning together in unison in a clockwise direction.

Bring your awareness back to the room that you are in, keep your eyes closed but begin to wiggle your fingers and toes. Take a deep breath in and out and slowly open your eyes.

Enjoy feeling clear and re-energised. You can repeat this meditation as often as you wish.

Aura readings

An aura is the energy field surrounding all living things and non-living objects. For most people it can be difficult to see auras with their physical eyes. There are seven main auric layers that wrap around the body or object in big circles of colour. Every aura is unique and individual, just as each person's fingerprints are.

The history of people seeing auras or knowing of auras goes back thousands of years. The use of energy and being able to see the aura has been used by Northern American shamans right through to Tibetan Buddhist monks. In the West we call the energy field around us an aura but it's called *Prana* in India and *Chi* in China.

Many of the European artists in the Middle Ages would paint the religious saints, angels, Jesus, Mary and along with deities with halos of light around their heads. Also many indigenous artworks from different cultures show primitive paintings or carvings of beings or people with circles of light around their heads.

Young children and babies can see auras more easily than adults. If you watch a baby when they first see or meet a person they usually don't look at the person's face or eyes. They look up above the person's forehead or head. Babies and young children can tell by looking at a person's aura or by feeling their energy if the person is positive or negative or if they are safe for them. If babies or children are unsure of a person's energy they usually will not go to them.

As with many psychic skills many children begin to close down or tune out of their psychic gifts, including seeing auras as they grow older and attend school. I have tried to teach my three children to keep their psychic senses open and have taught them from a young age about auras.

In many schools the teachers often say to the children to keep in their own personal bubble or space. The old saying this is my space and that is your space, can be applied with auras. Think of the aura as a large energy bubble with many layers.

The aura around living things such as people, plants or animals constantly changes every few minutes, just as our emotions constantly change.

At some mind, body, spirit festivals or New Age shops there are people who have special cameras which take photographs of your aura. The aura photograph is very interesting as it shows the different auric layers and colours around the person.

These aura photographs are great to be able to see what is going on around the person and to see what is coming in by looking at the colours and the shapes and fluidity of the auric layers. Sometimes there will be little bubbles or circles of light high up in the auric layers in the aura photographs. These circles or bubbles are a snapshot of spirit orbs of passed loved ones, angels or spirit guides around the person.

I usually try to get my aura photograph taken at least once every two years. It is amazing to see the differences every year. The colours and layers that you see in your aura photograph are a snapshot of that particular moment in time.

When you look at the aura around a non-living item such as a chair or coin it usually doesn't change. By looking at the human aura you can see the person's vitality, mental activity and health. The aura can also show disease in a person's body. The colour of the person's aura is often an indicator of the health of the person or the emotions that the person is feeling. If the colours are crisp and clean, the person should be feeling bright, positive and focused. When the colours are darker or muddier in colour the person may be ill, depressed, on heavy medication, or taking drugs or alcohol.

There are many different layers of the aura and I will focus on the most commonly known seven layers.

The seven aura layers

First layer — the etheric (first/root chakra)

Physical layer

The etheric layer is the first layer. It shows signs of illness and physical injury.

This is the layer that most people see or know about; it is also the easiest layer to see with your physical eyes. It can often be seen as a thin white band that is around 1.5 centimetres wide. It fits snugly to the body and follows the body's contours.

Second layer — the emotional body (second/sacral chakra)

Physical layer

The emotional body is the second layer. It shows what is happening with the person's emotions. This layer resembles the shape of the body and is around 5 centimetres to 10 centimetres. The colours may swirl and change to different colours of the rainbow as the person's emotions change.

Third layer — the mental body (third/ solar plexus chakra)

Physical layer

The mental body is the third layer. It is where a person's belief systems and personal power are highlighted. Mental health issues can be seen in this layer. This layer is usually a bright yellow colour and is visible around the shoulders and head. It stretches out 10 to 20 centimetres from the body.

Fourth layer — the astral layer (fourth/ heart chakra)
Bridge to the spiritual layer

The astral layer is the fourth layer and it is the layer of love, relationships and balance in life.

This layer is pink in colour and is the bridge between the physical and spiritual auric layers. It is located around 20 to 30 centimetres from the body. The astral layer shows a person's spiritual nature.

Fifth layer — the etheric template (fifth/throat chakra)
Spiritual layer

The etheric template is the fifth layer. It is the layer of inner identity and uniqueness, creativity and spiritual connection. This layer is like a negative of a photo. It has an open space of colour between it and the sixth layer, the celestial layer. It is located around 30 to 60 centimetres from the body.

Sixth layer — the celestial (sixth/ third eye chakra)
Spiritual layer

The celestial body is the sixth layer and is the layer of clairvoyance, unconditional love and connection with higher spiritual energies. This layer is made up of light pastel colours. This is the layer that you feel the highest levels of love and spiritual happiness. It is located around 60 to 90 centimetres from the body.

Seventh layer — The ketheric template 'casual body' (seventh/crown chakra)

Spiritual layer

The ketheric template is the seventh layer and it is the layer of that holds information about our soul contracts and past lives — our akashic records. This layer is gold or silver in colour. The ketheric template is where a person becomes one with their God or Goddess/Spirit; where they can become one with the Universe around them. It is located around 90 centimetres to 1.5 metres from the body.

Aura colours

Each colour that can be seen in the aura means a different thing. I have written my own interpretation of what each colour means to me on pp. 109–110.

You may find you have your own meanings for each colour. Before you read my list, write down what each colour means to you, for example, green means healing to me but it may mean something different to you. There are no right or wrong answers. Remember to go with the first thing you sense or feel for each colour.

Red

_____

_____

Blue

_____

_____

Black

_____

_____

Green

_____

_____

Yellow

_____

_____

Orange

_____

_____

Pink

_____

_____

Grey

_____

_____

Purple

_____

_____

White

_____

_____

Grey

_____

_____

Brown

_____

_____

My interpretation of aura colours

Black

Negativity, depression, alcohol or drug use.

Red

High energy; either positive or negative depending on the colour of red and how clear or murky it is. Fiery passion, fear or anger.

Yellow

Success, creativeness, intelligence.

Green

Healing, peace, relaxation.

Blue

Spiritually searching, growing intuition, protection.

Purple

Very psychically connected, protection, healing and open to spirit.

White

Indicates purity and/or protection; sometimes spirit guides show up as white orbs.

Pink

Affection, love, enjoyment.

Orange

Confidence, ambition, pride, creativity.

Brown

Confusion or discouragement.

Healthy and unhealthy auras

There are various things that can contribute to weakening your aura. They are as follows:

» *alcohol*

» *poor diet*

» *lack of fresh air*

» *drugs, cigarettes*

» *improper psychic activity, for example, Ouija boards and opening up your psychic ability too quickly*

» *negativity*

» *stress, both physical and mental*

» *lack of sleep*

» *lack of exercise*

» *lack of sunlight*

» *loneliness, lack of intimacy.*

Obviously the reverse of all of the above things help to strengthen your aura. These are as follows:

» *healthy diet and nutrition*

» *adequate sleep and exercise*

» *time outdoors in fresh air and sunlight*

» *meditation*

» *relaxation techniques*

» *creativity*

» *passion*

» *love and friendships*

» *happiness*

» *balanced mind and chakras.*

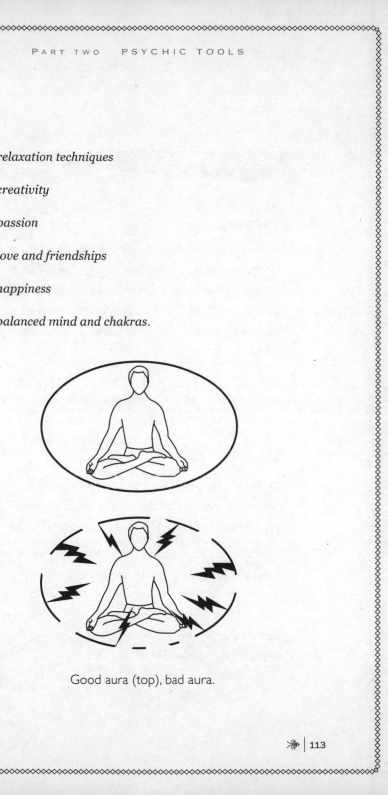

Good aura (top), bad aura.

The dark aura

I remember one of the first things that one of my friends/spiritual teachers taught me. It was that I had to look at people's auras and sense whether I was to read for that person or not. She told me that if I saw a dark aura around someone or felt a very heavy feeling around the person's energy I was not to read for them.

I listened to her at the time and thought on it for a while. It was not until sometime later that I asked her why I should not read someone with a very dark energy or aura. She told me that it would be incredibly draining for me to read someone like that.

This was very interesting for me to think about. I filed that information away and it wasn't until a a few years later that I finally understood what she had meant.

It was during a normal day of readings in the local shop that I used to work out of that I came across my first client that had an incredibly dark aura and negative energy. I had read a few people that day and it was almost lunchtime when this client came in. She had booked in a few weeks prior so it was expected that I would read for her.

When this client came and sat down everything started off as usual. I began by introducing myself and explaining how I read. I looked at the woman and she was barely sitting on the chair. Her eyes were half closed and she had her long hair dangling over her face.

As I looked at her I could feel in the pit of my stomach a very sick feeling and a tightness that made me feel very uncomfortable. I was not to be swayed as I wanted to help this woman and she obviously wanted some information and help as she was there for a reading, or so I thought!

As I began to read for her, she started to interrupt everything I was saying. Her eyes would become intense and she would begin to talk quite aggressively over me. This woman was in her mid to late thirties and I was only in my early twenties.

When I told her what I was picking up around her psychically she began to get more agitated. It was then that I had remembered what my friend had taught me. I looked up at the woman and tried to see her aura, all the while still feeling sick in my stomach.

In her aura I felt a very thick dark smoky energy. This was not unexpected. The woman smelt of alcohol and strong cigarettes. This was a big learning lesson in my life. The first lesson was to listen to others who have experience, the second lesson was to listen to my guides and the third lesson was to protect myself and not let my ego think it is always right.

To cut a long story short, I ended up telling the woman that I would give her a refund because I did not feel it was right to continue with the reading. She was very angry and abusive when I told her this but it was the right thing for me to do.

After reading for her I was quite ill for the rest of the day and the two days following. The negativity had affected my own aura and it was a few days before I felt back to my normal self.

I am not saying that you should avoid people with heaviness in their auras as each of us go through trials and tribulations which would make our own auras muddy or perhaps a bit darker in colour. Just be aware that other people's energy can affect your own and if you are a healer or reader, be mindful of this when you are doing your spiritual work.

Aura exercises

You don't have to be a professional psychic or healer to be able to see auras. Everyone has the ability to be able to use their sixth sense and this includes seeing auras. Sometimes it just takes practice and or finding the right exercise that works for you. I have taught this exercise for many years and I have to say at least 90 per cent of my students can see at least the etheric auric layer very quickly.

 SEE YOUR OWN AURA

1 First relax your mind and breathe deeply.

2 Place your hand on piece of plain white paper.

3 Close your eyes, then very slowly begin to open them just until your eyes are barely open and you are squinting.

4 With your eyes squinting focus on your hands. Look at the space between your fingers.

Notice the white fuzzy band of light around your fingers and hand. This is the first auric layer, the etheric layer.

You can do this same exercise with any object or living thing. Trees are great to look at as they have amazing auras and don't run away from you like animals or pets do.

 FEEL YOUR OWN AURA

1 Relax and breathe deeply.

2 Place your hands together with your palms touching, as in a prayer position.

3 Slowly begin to rub your hands together at chest height. Keep rubbing your hands together until you feel that your hands are warm.

4 When you are ready very slowly begin to pull your hands apart to less than two centimetres. You should begin to feel a pull between your hands. If you don't feel the pull, begin to rub your hands together again. Keep trying until you feel the resistance between your hands.

5 If you can feel the energy between both of your hands, have fun with it. See how far apart you can pull your hands before the energy breaks.

6 When you have your hands close together you can feel your aura bouncing off each hand. It should feel squashy or like magnets repelling each other.

Note: You can do this exercise in a group. Have one person in the middle with a blindfold with other people around them standing still. The person in the middle has to sense if the person in front of them is male or female, and feel the energy with their hands not physically touching the people.

 SEE OTHER PEOPLE'S AURAS

1 Find a partner to work with you on this exercise.

2 Try to find a blank wall or light coloured wall for one of you to sit against. If you can't find a blank wall use a light coloured sheet or piece of paper and tape it to the wall.

3 Sit facing each other with one of you sitting with your back against the blank wall. The person who is sitting against the wall needs to sit calmly and close their eyes.

4 You will take turns at seeing each other's auras. It is easier for the person who is against the wall to just relax with their eyes closed, so that they don't distract the other person.

5. The person who is trying to see the aura needs to relax their mind and breathe deeply. The person needs to close their eyes and very slowly begin to open their eyes just until their eyes are barely open and are squinting.

6. It's important that when you are trying to see an aura around a person you don't try and focus too much. By looking at the other person's shoulder height and to the left or right side it can help you to see their aura.

7. If the person is having problems seeing the aura, repeat the process. Slowly open the eyes and close them again. See what colours appear in the third eye/ mind or what colours are felt by the person seeing the aura. Once you have noticed a colour in the aura you should then go ahead and see if the colour is dull or vibrant. Is it smooth or spiky?

8. Not everyone sees auras with their physical eyes. Many people feel auras or see them with their eyes closed.

9. When the first person has seen the partner's aura, write or draw what you have seen or experienced

when looking at the other person's aura, then swap places and repeat the process.

AUTOMATIC WRITING

Automatic writing is when a person is receiving information psychically, either clairvoyantly or clairaudiently and they write this information down. This information that the person is receiving does not come from the conscious thought of the writer as it comes from an external energy such as spirit guides, passed loved ones or other spiritual entities.

The information that is given to the person psychically contains important information that relates to the person or people around them. Pictures may also be drawn.

There are some particular times that automatic writing is very helpful, for example, it may be an uplifting inspirational message to help the person through tough times, or it may be a clue to a future event such as a particular date or day that a new job or relationship may come into the person's life. Another reason that some people do automatic writing is to receive messages and to connect with their spirit guides or their passed loved ones.

With the invention of typewriters and computers we are now not just limited to automatic writing; you can also do automatic typing. It is the same process as automatic writing except you type everything that you hear or see instead of writing it with a pen or pencil.

When you first start to learn automatic writing it can be difficult to know if it is your own thoughts that you are hearing. It can also be hard to relax and to trust in the information that you are receiving.

I like to connect with my spirit guides via automatic writing on a regular basis. It is good for me to connect in this way because I like to ask specific questions of my spirit guides and keep a record of what they have said. It can be quite hard to read the writing after I have finished automatic writing because I write differently when I have my eyes closed and I am channelling. My normal writing tends to be quite messy and swirly with the letters of a similar size and quite close together. When I do automatic writing my writing is very messy and on a very sharp slant to the right, completely different handwriting than my own.

I know when it is my spirit guides that are giving me information to write because they always tend to use the same type of phrases and words that I normally would never use in my everyday speech or writing. My spirit guides also give me a particular physical feeling of a pulling in my stomach when they want to get my attention and they want me to sit down and do some writing.

Many famous writers, poets and musicians have in fact channelled or automatically written their works. They may not be aware of this but I do feel that they were guided by their specialist spirit guides to help them create their amazing pieces.

I actually channelled a lot of my second book *What happens next? Answering your questions about life after death*. I would have the feeling that I would have to write something down and I would sit with a pen and paper and write everything down that my spirit guides told me to. I wrote the book over many years during different writing sessions and often had no idea why I was writing about certain things until many years later.

The process of automatic writing is very relaxing for me. I like to make sure that I am not going to be disturbed and I sit down and ask my spirit guides to come forward. I then have a pen in my hand and a large piece of plain paper.

When I first tried automatic writing all I could do was draw swirls and circles and no words came out at all. It is important that you persevere with it because it does take practice.

A big tip that I can offer you is that you may like to try to keep your eyes closed when you are writing because it can help you to concentrate on what you are hearing clairaudiently.

AUTOMATIC WRITING EXERCISE

1 To begin to do automatic writing try to make sure that you won't be disturbed. You may like to close the curtains or blinds and light a candle or some of your favourite incense to add to the atmosphere.

2 It's important that you call upon your spirit guides, angels, god or goddesses, passed loved ones or whoever you want to communicate with for your automatic writing. Ask them to give you any information that you need and to keep you protected in the white light or whatever psychic protection you would like to use for yourself. Go with the flow with what you hear in thought form or experience and keep your thoughts relaxed.

3 When you are relaxed pick up the pen and paper, close your eyes and listen to what thoughts come into your mind. The thoughts will come in your own voice most of the time and they will come through very quickly. Make sure that you write the thoughts down as soon as you hear them.

4 Don't stop to read what you have written until the end because it breaks the flow of the information that you are receiving. When you are not hearing any more pieces of information or feeling the need to write anymore, stop writing. Thank your guides or spirit helpers—whoever was working with you—and relax.

5 Try and read what you have written. It can be tricky at first if your writing is messy but you should remember parts of what you have written while it is still fresh in your mind. I like to put a date at the top of the page so that I know when the information was channelled and I keep any significant writings to look at in the future.

6 You may like to have a drink of water to ground your energy after doing automatic writing because it can be draining.

Congratulations on doing automatic writing. Next time you may like to write down very specific questions beforehand and ask them of your spirit guides.

PART
THREE

Psychic Skills

Extra sensory perception (ESP)/sixth sense

Most of us have all five senses (except in the case of a disability or being visually or hearing impaired). These five senses relate to feeling, smelling, tasting, seeing and hearing. These five senses are what are considered normal. Extra sensory perception or ESP is anything that is experienced or any knowledge that is gained outside of these five senses. It is from another sense—a sixth sense—which is where the term extra sensory perception comes from. ESP gives the person information about the past, present or future. The term ESP usually refers to the main psychic skills:

» *Mental telepathy is being able to communicate with another person without using the five senses.*

» *Clairvoyance is being able to perceive things from the past, present or future.*

» *Clairaudience is the ability to hear sounds with and without the physical ears.*

» *Precognition is seeing or knowing about future events without using the five senses.*

» *Retrocognition is seeing or knowing about*

*events that have occurred in the past without
using the five senses*

» *Psychometry is receiving information from
holding a personal object without using the
five senses.*

There are many more psychic skills that the sixth sense
or ESP relates to but mental telepathy, clairvoyance and
precognition are the most commonly known and studied
categories. As you go through this book I will go into each
area in more detail so that you can learn more about each of
these psychic skills.

MENTAL TELEPATHY

Mental telepathy is communication between two separate
minds. This communication can be in the form of
feelings, mental images, thoughts or ideas. It is a form of
communication without using speech and without using the
five senses. Mental telepathy is often called a sixth sense. By
using the sixth sense a person can communicate with the
other person without talking to them on the phone or being
in visual sight or in the same room. Mental telepathy is also
known as telepathy. Telepathy comes from the Greek word
'tele' meaning distant/remote and 'pathe' meaning feeling
or awareness.

For telepathic communication to occur there has to be two people: one person has to be the sender and send the message and the other person has to be the receiver, the person who picks up on the message or information that is being sent.

Throughout the ages in many different tribal societies telepathy is instinctual and is a vital survival mechanism that is encouraged and practiced from birth. In developed countries and cities the concept of being able to use telepathic communication has been long forgotten except for a small minority of people who are realising that they can use their intuition (ESP) to develop themselves and help others spiritually.

The strongest form of telepathic communication is between family members, lovers and very close friends. If you spend a lot of time with someone you become more in tune with their energies. In the case of family and friends you adjust your energy frequency to match theirs. This forms a psychic link and allows you to communicate telepathically.

Usually women are considered to be more psychic or telepathic in families rather than the men. This may be because women are sometimes more open to sensitive and spiritual things. It could also be the mother's instinct and psychic bond that occurs once you have been pregnant or given birth to a child.

Many times a family member or friend will sense something that is going to happen just before it happens, such as an accident or illness. Often the family member or friend (the sender) will send a warning feeling or message to the receiver. If the receiver is linked in or open to the message an accident could be avoided or travel plans changed, just in the nick of time.

Some people are really great at sending telepathic messages and others are great receivers. Not everyone can do both. It can take practice to get to know how to send and receive telepathic images or messages.

The stronger the emotion, the stronger the telepathic communication generally. In times of great need or distress the energy and emotion behind the message will often be felt a lot more clearly then in just a normal everyday event.

I find it's always a good idea to practice telepathic games with your children from a very young age. Playing telepathic games helps to keep the psychic bond between you and keep the link open. Start by playing simple games such as what colour and shape am I thinking of? The child has to try and see what you are sending them and vice versa.

Some humans can also communicate telepathically with animals. Often you will hear of dogs and pets that have saved their owner's life or have alerted their owner of some danger. Pets have very strong psychic awareness and can often sense things that humans can't; they will try to warn their owners of dangerous situations.

Telepathy exercise

Obviously with this exercise you will need at least two people, a receiver and a sender. I like to use two people to start off with as it is easier to focus than having too many senders or receivers.

TELEPATHY EXERCISE

1 The first thing you need to do is find five images that you would like to focus upon for this exercise. You may like to draw a circle, a square, a triangle, a rectangle and a star. It is easier to use very plain shapes that are well known to start off with. You may like to colour each shape or image in one colour such as a red circle, blue square, green triangle, yellow rectangle and purple star.

2 Choose one person to be the sender and the other person to be the receiver for the first turn. The sender needs to focus on one of the images without letting the other person see the image that they are looking at. When the sender starts to send the image telepathically he or she needs to let the receiver know.

(3) The receiver needs to sit quietly and see what image they can feel, see or sense that the sender is sending to them. It can be helpful to have the drawings in front of them of what the shapes and colours are.

(4) The receiver should then tell the sender what they felt the shape or colour was. The sender should let the receiver know if they were right or not with the colour or shape.

(5) Usually I get my students to try this exercise three times in a row and then they swap over to be the receiver or sender.

It's interesting to note that when I have taught this exercise in a workshop environment some people are really good receivers and some are great senders. I have also noticed that some people are more in tune with certain people's energy and they get three out of three right when they do this exercise, but when they move on to another person they may only get one right or none at all. This is because it takes two people to work together for telepathy to work. Some people are more open than others and can send and receive more easily.

Another thing that often happens when I teach this exercise is how connected siblings or family members are. I have had family members come to my workshops before and I have placed them together for this exercise. When they are together they often will get two or three out of three right. This is because family members, partners and very close friends are often already on the same telepathic wavelength. After I put the family members together I then separate them and put them with someone who they don't know. Usually they don't have the same success rate that they had with their family member or person that they know.

CLAIRVOYANCE

Clairvoyance (clear seeing) is being able to perceive things such as a person's aura, image, symbol or event that may have occurred in the past or present, or may occur in the future. A person who is clairvoyant will see this information with their inner eye/third eye, not with their physical eyes. If you are clairvoyant you can perceive things a lot more clearly and have greater insight into things that are not physically visible around you.

To explain it a little more clearly, clairvoyance is like having your eyes closed and you are looking at your own kind of movie screen in your mind. When looking at a symbol or an event it is like watching a movie or having a memory. Sometimes it is as simple as a picture or word popping into your mind.

One example I like to give to my students when teaching about clairvoyance is how random some of the symbols or information is sometimes. Sometimes you will be shown a symbol or picture and you will think 'what is that for?' I remember years ago I was reading for a lady who was quite hard to read for. She was determined not to let her guard down. The lady sat with her arms crossed and just stared at me during the whole reading. I was very young at that time and it was difficult for me to keep having the courage to keep reading for her. Even though I was giving her exact names and times and answering all of her questions, she just wouldn't let up her energy to enjoy the process. In desperation I asked my spirit guides to please give me a big piece of information that would definitely confirm to this lady that the information is correct and give me a bit of confirmation to relax more. Do you know what my spirit guides showed me clairvoyantly? A washing machine!

As soon as I saw the image of a washing machine I just about lost my nerve and had an internal mental yell at my spirit guides. I asked them why they wanted to embarrass me and why they would just simply show me a washing machine. They just kept showing me this and all the while the lady in front of me had no idea that I had this internal mental conversation going on.

Eventually I gave in to my spirit guides and trusted them, as I usually do. I took a deep breath and said, 'I see a washing machine for you. I know it sounds weird but I feel it's important.' It was amazing. The lady unfolded her arms and finally smiled at me. She said, 'thank you that was the validation I needed. My washing machine actually broke down just before I came here today and no one knows this. I wanted to see if you were telling me the truth and now I know you are. I can now take on board all of the other information you have told me today.' It was that simple!

CLAIRAUDIENCE

Clairaudience (clear hearing) is the ability to hear sounds with and without using your physical ears. The sounds may be in the form of voices talking, music playing or a high-pitched ringing sound. There are two types of clairaudience — objective and subjective.

Objective clairaudience means that you can hear the sound with your physical ears and often more than one person at a time can hear the sound, for example, there have been times when I have heard loud footsteps walking down my hallway with my physical ears and my husband has heard it as well. (There wasn't anybody walking down the hallway at the time, it was a spirit person, trying to get our attention.)

Subjective clairaudience is when you can hear an internal voice or sound that no one else can hear but you. Often it can be confusing at first trying to work out if it's your own thoughts or a message coming through because usually you will hear the voice in your own thought voice.

There are some cases when I have heard a different voice but usually it's my own thought voice.

Word of warning

I know this may sound silly but I feel it's important to mention here that there are some medical conditions such as schizophrenia and multiple personality disorders where people do hear voices. There is a big difference between hearing voices from a medical perspective where the voices are uncontrollable and are often negative and the nurturing voice of your own spirit guides or intuitive higher self. If you feel like you may be having problems distinguishing between whether it's your spirit guides or a repetitive voice that is asking you to self-harm or harm others please seek medical advice from your medical professional as soon as possible.

A spirit guide would never ask you to harm another person or yourself. They can be bossy and pushy but they are still loving and supportive. Please use your common sense. If you hear something irrational or quite destructive such as 'go jump off the top of a building' without due reason, check first!

Often when you are first learning to connect with spirit you will hear things that you don't usually hear. The sounds that come through may come in the form of a quiet whisper that can sound like your own voice in thought form, or even a loud noise which gets your attention.

Spirit people/spirit guides can often sound like a radio that is out of tune or a budgie that is first learning to talk. It can be frustrating to hear the mumbled, squeaks at first, but try to persist as you get used to tuning your sixth sense/clairaudient hearing.

If you are hearing spirits and it is difficult for you to understand what they are saying, it can help if you ask them to step back from you. They may be trying too hard to get you to listen to them. There is nothing wrong with asking for what you need, and by asking them to step back it may help you to hear them more clearly. I know that this worked for me. Within a few days of asking my spirit guides to step further back, I could begin to make out words or sentences of what they were trying to say.

When you receive a message from spirit guides the information is not always delivered through one psychic skill. Often you will hear a message clairaudiently, then you will see a sign clairvoyantly with your third eye and you may also sense the spirit with your physical body. Spirit is very creative in the way that they try to communicate with you.

There is no right or wrong way to communicate with spirit. Some people are more in tune with their clairvoyant gifts while others may be more in tune with their clairsentience.

CLAIRSENTIENCE

Clairsentience (clear sensing and clear knowing) is the ability to feel things physically and to sense things that are out of the ordinary. A lot of people are clairsentient; it is one of the most common psychic gifts. To be clairsentient is to have a gut feeling or an inner knowing and to have physical confirmation through some of your other five senses.

Have you ever felt the hair on your arms stand up? Or felt shivers go through your body when you are thinking of something spooky, or you are talking about something and to confirm it you get the feeling in your body to stop and pay attention?

Often people will smell smoke, perfume or other specific scents that are spirits' ways of getting your attention. Obviously if you smell these things and people are around you who are smoking or wearing perfume, that is not a sign. But if you are in a room or in your home by yourself and you suddenly smell a particular scent that does not belong, stop and pay attention, and think who has passed away who may have been linked to that scent or smell.

I often will smell the aftershave Old Spice when I am at home by myself and when I need extra confirmation or help from spirit. My husband does not wear this aftershave and no one else is in the house. This was the aftershave my grandfather (Nonno) who has passed away wore and it is a sign that he is around.

Many of my clients have experienced clairsentience in the form of smelling the cigarette smoke that their dad used to smoke or the favourite perfume of their mum has passed away. I also know a psychic friend of mine who actually smells a really bad smell when she has to pay attention to something or be cautious — it is her spirit guide's way of warning her of something.

Sensory questionnaire — how do you sense the spirit world?

This is a quick exercise to help you start to look at how you sense the spirit world. There are no right or wrong answers here. Filling out this questionnaire may help you realise that you are already using your sixth sense.

Do you feel or sense spirits around you?

_____

_____

_____

_____

Have you or do you see spirits or shadows/shapes of people or animals?

_____

_____

_____

_____

_____

Have you seen spirit orbs (little circles of light) with your own physical eyes?

_____

_____

_____

_____

_____

Do you feel uncomfortable or uneasy in certain places that may have a lot of history or emotions attached to it?

_____

_____

_____

_____

Do you find yourself getting really drained around certain people or in large crowds?

_____

_____

_____

_____

_____

_____

Can you smell things like smoke, perfume, etc, around you that don't belong to you or anyone else around you?

_____

_____

_____

_____

_____

_____

Do you sometimes feel like you are intensely angry or upset after being around an angry person?

_____

_____

_____

_____

_____

_____

_____

_____

If someone else around you is feeling sick do you feel similar?

_____

_____

_____

_____

_____

_____

_____

_____

_____

Take note of how many of these questions you have answered yes to. Look at what your answers tell you. Are you using your sixth sense? Or are you relying mainly on your normal five senses seeing, hearing, tasting, smelling and touching. It is ok if you feel that you are using your five senses more than your sixth sense. By working through this book and opening yourself up more psychically, your sixth sense will become stronger and you will eventually use it more and more.

PSYCHOMETRY

One psychic skill that I like to use when doing my readings or mediumship connections is to use psychometry. Psychometry is holding a personal object in your hand to feel energy off it to sense very specific information about the owner of the object. The information you receive may come through clairvoyantly, clairaudiently, clairsentiently or a combination of all three. During a psychometric reading the psychic may experience emotions, sounds, tastes, scents and/or visions.

The best objects to use are a piece of jewellery, keys, purse, wallet, sunglasses or mobile phone. I like to make sure that the object has been on my client for at least half an hour to make sure there is enough energy on it. The closer the object has been to the person's body the better.

Some psychics also read by holding a piece of clothing or a photograph. Many times the police will give a psychic a piece of clothing or jewellery of a deceased or missing person so that they can gain some information which may help them solve their case.

Note: If the object has been owned by various people, for example, a piece of jewellery or watch that has been handed down it can hold residual energy from the previous owners. It can be easier when you are starting out to ask the person if the object has been owned by anyone else.

How does psychometry work?

Psychometry works because our bodies have a magnetic energy field, otherwise known as an aura (which you learnt about on p.101.) Whenever we come in contact with an object we unintentionally lay down information and energy onto that object.

The strong emotions such as love, passion, grief and anger seem to be the main energy that is often retained in an object. Psychics can pick up a lot of information by using psychometry; it can be a feeling, a time, a location, an event or a name.

I personally like to use psychometry at the beginning of my mediumship readings. When I hold a piece of the sitter's jewellery it helps me to link to their energy and it also helps their passed loved ones and spirit guides to come through with messages for them.

Note: When doing a reading using psychometry, always try to pick up the object with your non-dominant hand, (the hand that you don't usually write with).

If you use your dominant hand, you may leave your own energy imprint on the object unintentionally. (If you feel energy more strongly in your dominant hand it's ok to use that hand.)

Try not to practice psychometry on gemstones or crystals, as they have their own strong vibrations and it makes it harder to pick up the person's energy.

Remember it can take time to learn new skills, so please don't be put off or get too frustrated if you don't get your desired results on your first few times at practising psychometry.

 PSYCHOMETRY EXERCISE

1. Practice this exercise with a friend. Both of you should sit quietly and comfortably. If you wish to do a quick meditation you could do so at the beginning. Make sure that you have psychically shielded yourself and that you are grounded (from the earlier chapter on psychic protection on p37).

2. Place an object of your friend's in your non-dominant hand. Place your other hand lightly on top of the object.

3. Close your eyes and feel the energy of the object.

Is it warm or cold? Does it feel smooth or rough?

Let your mind stay relaxed and just go with the flow of the images you see or feel.

Do you have any physical sensations in your body?

Can you hear or sense any words or see any visual pictures for your friend?

Please don't doubt what you see. Verbalise what you are seeing to your friend. It may not make sense to you, but it may to them.

 Say everything you see, no matter how normal it looks, for example, remember the washing machine that I told you about earlier that I saw when I read for a lady? These small bits of information are important and they all form confirmations for you and the sitter. They help break down the barriers and let you and your sitter know that you are on the right track with your information.

Always trust what you see. Doubts and second guessing yourself can cause blocks so keep practising and don't give up. Remember there is no right or wrong way to use your psychic gifts.

SPIRIT SIGNS: WHAT SIGNS CAN I RECEIVE FROM THE SPIRIT WORLD?

Signs from your spirit guides or from passed loved ones come in many different ways. You may hear, see, sense or feel signs from the spirit world. It might be just a small sign, such as the lights flicking on and off, or you may have a physical feeling such as the hairs on your arms or back of your neck standing up very unexpectedly.

Some other very common spirit signs are white feathers being left in front of you or on the floor in very obscure places where birds would never be, constantly finding coins as you walk along, and butterflies, birds or dragonflies that seem to linger and follow you.

Nature signs through animals, birds, insects or even trees, clouds, etc. are some of the most powerful signs and messengers that you can get. Many indigenous cultures have such a great affinity with nature and what each of the different animal behaviours and signs mean.

I want you to be able to make your own dictionary of signs and symbols. It is important that you take in any information that you learn from others and put your own spin on it. What may mean something to someone else in a sign or symbol may mean something completely different to you. For example, many people believe that black crows are a bad omen or sign when they appear and they feel that it may mean a death is coming in the family. I do not believe this. The black crow to me means a messenger, that there is a sign coming to me soon and I need to pay attention.

From my experience I have found that my spirit guides like to show me things in three different ways in a short amount of time. They will always try and get their message across to me but because I am a human I sometimes don't pick up on all of their signs or messages, so they need to show me things more than once to get my attention.

One of my favourite examples of how my spirit guides were trying to get my attention one day is to do with yoga. I remember one day, years ago, I was driving and I stopped at the lights and next to me was a bus stop. On the bus stop were a lot of different flyers and posters that were flapping in the breeze. I remember looking over and noticing one flyer in particular and it was advertising a local yoga class. I didn't think much about it, the traffic lights changed and I continued driving. I ended up driving a bit further up the road and was listening to the radio in the car when I heard a new ad come on the air. The ad was for a new gym that was opening and they were advertising their yoga classes. I listened to the ad and thought nothing much of it and continued driving.

Later that day I went to my children's school to pick them up. Well, you would never guess what happened. School finished and my two older kids walked up to my car and jumped in. My eldest son Lachie said to me, 'Hey Mum, why don't you do yoga anymore?' It was the first thing out of his mouth, no quick hellos or anything. I laughed to myself and had a quick mental conversation with my spirit guides and said, 'Thank you, I get the message'.

My spirit guides had wanted me to go back to doing yoga. They had gone out of their way to show me in three separate ways what they wanted. Now if only I had noticed one or two of these signs it might not have made much sense to me but because I noticed the three signs and knew how my spirit guides work it was easier for me to understand what they wanted. They do things in quirky ways that get your attention in a short amount of time. Each person will feel their signs in different ways and their spirit guides or passed loved ones will communicate in different ways. It can take some time to learn about how spirit communicates with you and what the signs around you mean.

Certainly you need to be careful not to assume that every little thing that happens is a sign, but it helps if you are open-minded and accept that there might be a reason these things are occurring around you.

The big Queensland flood, Brisbane 2011

Early in 2011, I experienced one of the biggest natural disasters in my city's and country's history. The disaster was made up of flooding far north of my city in north Queensland, flooding north of my city of Brisbane and a big inland tsunami that hit the country towns a few hours away from us. The devastation was massive; three-quarters of Queensland was flooded, an area the size of Germany and France together.

After relentless rainfall the dams and river systems could not cope so the flooding headed down the river towards our homes and city. There were warnings on the media, TV, radio. Evacuation was needed in many suburbs. As we lived close to the city and quite close to many of the suburbs that were highlighted to be flooded and evacuated I was really worried about the safety of my family, our home and work.

Twenty people lost their lives and many were missing. Thousands and thousands of people lost all of their belongings, their homes and their businesses. The damage was so extensive that it was as if a war had ripped through the state. Roads, food, water and electricity were cut off in many places for days.

The reason I am telling you about this event is that there were signs that I was shown before this flood that did help me and my family. I had received signs for the past five or so years that it was going to happen. My spirit guides had told me that the eastern seaboard of Australia would be hit with high tides like tsunamis and mass flooding.

Each time my husband and I thought about moving houses I would mention this to my husband and we would reconsider where we were looking at buying. I even spoke to my family and friends and warned them in as casual a way as I could. I especially warned my mother who lives with her husband on an island in the middle of Moreton Bay. Each time a storm came I would worry for the people who lived right on the coast or for my mum who lived on the island.

I am not the only one who felt this though as many people I had met through my work or through various different spiritual groups shared the same vision. They felt that the waters were going to rise and felt the need to move up high or to live away from any water sources that may flood.

Even though my spirit guides gave me this warning I was still very scared and not sure if my house would go under in the water or not. We often have flooding under our house and backyard during heavy rains.

When I heard on the radio what happened with the inland tsunami so close to Brisbane and how it was going to affect Brisbane with flooding. I searched within and asked my spirit guides for signs of survival.

The first thing I felt was that this was going to be a huge event and would not pass by suddenly. It would be a time of having to stop everything and bunker down. My energy was jumpy and I knew that I had to put things into place quite quickly.

I called my manager and asked him to move all of my readings I had booked in for that day, perhaps moving the whole week. I tried to explain to him that even if the flood was not going to hit us yet or if at all I could not read because the energy was too scattered and I was too worried. The next thing I did was to call my husband to tell him to get our two older children who were on the other side of the city at his parents' place. He told me he couldn't get them because he had to stay at work and told me to leave them there as they would be safe up high on top of a hill.

Our little girl was at daycare. My husband told me to leave her there and to see how the day panned out because the flood might not even happen. My guides and my gut instincts told me differently.

I hung up the phone and within minutes my neighbour Sarah who is also my friend who is very psychic called me and asked me where my kids were. I told her where the boys were and that Lilli my daughter was at daycare. She told me she felt I should go and get Lilli straightaway. This flood was going to happen and she felt that, as I did, that it was going to be a big thing.

That was yet another sign for me. I got into my car and asked my spirit guides again to help me see my way clear to know what to do. In times of panic it can be hard to know if it is just fear or in fact a sign. I always ask for more than one sign for confirmations.

As I was in the car driving down my street towards Lilli's daycare a white minivan pulled out in front of me. I was shocked that it pulled out so fast until I saw what was written on the back windscreen of the car and all over the side of the car. The writing said 'Flood Damage Cleaning 24 hours — all carpets and upholstery'. This was my second sign. What were the chances of that minivan pulling out in front of me? I was more than ever determined to get Lilli and get home to prepare for what needed to be done. When I arrived at the daycare centre all of the teachers were surprised to see me as Lilli had only been dropped off an hour earlier by my husband. I explained what I was doing and what I felt and thankfully they listened to me.

The director of the daycare centre said she would put the parents on alert that they may have to come and pick up their children early due to the potential storm or flooding.

The third sign came from nature for me. There was no rain or loud thunder, but the energy felt very heavy and still. It felt like the calm before the storm. There were no birds in my yard; it was incredibly quiet. Usually we have all types of birds that fly in and around our home and they are very vocal.

I remembered what one of my Native American friends had told me about how animals react and forewarn you in natural disasters. The animals will often move to higher land or bunker down, even before a drop of rain comes or anything begins to shake she told me. I listened and heard the silence and this was my third sign.

That was enough warning for me. I packed Lilli in the car, went straight to the shops, and loaded up on water and essential items. By the time I came home the flooding had already started rising around Brisbane and I could not get down to the southside to get my sons. They had to stay with their grandparents.

We were blessed and were one of the lucky families. Our house and work were spared. We were cut off from family and friends, the city and supplies for a while, but we were safe. We were able to drive through the night to get our sons before we were cut off.

I have thanked my spirit guides and the Universe for keeping my family and friends safe. Had we moved to some of the areas we were looking at buying we would have had water over the roof and would have nothing left. I have also asked the Universe to provide shelter, love, support and healing to those affected.

Please know that the reason I am sharing this with you all is not to say that other people should have listened to their guides or that we are in anyway extra special. I was just lucky that I had been taught to listen to my spirit guides and to look for signs.

Remember that signs may come years or months ahead to warn you and you may not understand them at the time. I had thought that the floods would come from a tsunami from the ocean and flooding from the ocean. But it hadn't;

it had come from an inland tsunami, the likes of something that has never been seen before here. It was my personal take on it that said the ocean.

The other thing to remember is that you must always check on your signs and ask for extra confirmation like I did.

HOW TO TURN OFF OR MANAGE
YOUR PSYCHIC ABILITY

I believe that each person is born with their own intuition and psychic ability, it is just that some people are unaware of their intuition or do not wish to enhance their intuition. A lot of people are born with a natural psychic ability that is quite advanced and it allows them to see, hear, feel or sense things in the spiritual world. This may be a good thing for you as you may want to develop your intuition, but some people look at it as a negative or a scary thing.

Often I have people that come to me that ask me how to turn off their psychic gifts. They don't want to know what is going to happen, they don't want to be able to feel things so much. This is quite a common thing. They are scared of what they are feeling or seeing and just want to be left alone to be happy with a normal life.

I can understand what they are going through. I have been through this at various times throughout my life as well. It can be incredibly difficult having to buffer yourself from other people's feelings and thoughts all the time.

When I was first learning to deal with being a medium I would get hassled all the time by spirits, day and night. I would be in the shower washing my hair and would be scared to close my eyes to rinse my hair because I could feel so many other spirits in the bathroom with me. Looking back it is funny, but at the time it wasn't.

I would be in the line at the local supermarket waiting to pay for my groceries and a spirit would start talking to me, telling me about the person in the line in front of me, asking me to pass a message on to them. Of course I couldn't speak to the person as they would have thought I was nuts.

At parties, school functions for my kids, even during private moments with my family I would have to try and keep focused on what I was doing because of all the distractions around me of the spirit people trying to talk to me. I was like a seven-eleven shop — open all hours to any passing spirit who saw my light and wanted to come and say hi or pass on a message.

After a while I said enough was enough and that I needed to have as normal a life as possible. My life is still not exactly normal but I had to try and make some ground rules. I said to my spirit guides that if they didn't do something about all these spirits hassling me I would not do any spiritual work. I would just totally disregard all things spiritual. I put my foot down and demanded to be in control of whom and what I was working with spiritually. It was the best thing that I could have done. I said to my spirit guides that I didn't want any extra spirits coming in around me unless I have asked them to. My spirit guides told me to put a trigger in place that would let them know or other spirits know when it was ok for them to come in.

My trigger for my spirit guides is that firstly I have to ask for them to come forwards (except in times of emergencies or great need), and I have to have specific crystals and/or another psychic tool such as oracle cards or a pendulum, etc. This worked really well for me and still does today. I no longer need to have the crystals or other psychic tools. I just ask my spirit guides straight out and I trust that they will do what I ask.

If you would like to close down your psychic gift or control it to feel more secure you can set a trigger of your own to work with your spirit guides. You may ask for it to be shut down for now, just until you can deal with it better. Or you may ask for your children's gifts to be toned down or shut down (except for emergencies) so that they can concentrate more on school or sleep better. Your child's spirit guides will know when to open them back up again. My spirit guides shut me down during school and opened me up again when I was seventeen.

You can ask for your spirit guides to step back for a while to give you space. They will not be offended by this. In times of great stress of physical illness they understand that you need to be able to feel comfortable. They will still be around you; they just won't be psychically making themselves known as much.

PART
FOUR

Spirit Guides

What are spirit guides?

Everyone has their own spirit guides; some people just are not aware that they exist or are not open to their guides. Most people usually have approximately five spirit guides, but this number can vary as some guides come and go at different times in your life. Each guide has a specific purpose to help you with, for example, a healing guide, a clairvoyant guide, a guide for life changes, a creative guide for artists, and so on.

Your main spirit guide (or master guide as they are sometimes called) stays with you from birth to your passing. You make an agreement with this main guide before you are born and decide that you will work together in this life and map out what you would like to achieve and work through. You may have known your main guide in a previous life as they may have been your mother, brother, sister or friend.

Your spirit guides love you very much and would never harm you or do anything that isn't in your best interest. They are the greatest best friends you could ever have. They can be quite cheeky and have a funny sense of humour too.

Spirit guides will not make decisions for you. This is your life and they aren't allowed, nor do they want to tell you how to live it. If you ask for their advice they will happily give it to you, but the final decision is ultimately yours to make. Sometimes they will give you advice that you don't really understand at the time, but later it will all make sense and become another piece of the puzzle of your life.

Many people I meet focus too much on finding out their guides' names and what they look like and what nationality they are. It's not important to know your guides' names.

A lot of the time people ask me why so many people have Native American guides or Tibetan Monk guides. The reason for this is that many of these ancient and spiritual cultures have always been very spiritually advanced and have been in touch with Mother Earth and spirituality for many thousands of years. Therefore, a lot more of these people have come back to help and share their experience with us.

It is important to note that your guides will appear in a form that they know you can relate to. An example of this is my main guide. He is Native American and his name is Running Grey Wolf. Now he appears to me as an older Native American man and this is a form that I can relate to as I have a love of the Native American culture and spirituality.

Some guides may choose not to show themselves visually. This is their choice; they may prefer to only allow you to hear them in your inner ear. Or they may give you a sensation you can relate to them and you may only feel them. Each guide will have a different feel to them.

When you first start to communicate with your spirit guides try not to rush it. Remember that all friendships and relationships take time to develop and to get to know each other. If you rush this you may run the risk of getting frustrated and annoyed, making it counterproductive. I always suggest trying to feel out your guides first.

Many times you may have already felt your spirit guides without even knowing it. Sometimes you may feel a subtle physical change or feeling which you may not realise is your spirit guide trying to get your attention, such as heat on one side of your face, or pressure on the top of your head or in your brow area (third eye). You may even hear or think a thought in your mind which is something that you needed to know or something that doesn't make sense at first. If you have a thought and you don't remember thinking it, it is most probably your spirit guide, particularly if it is a piece of information that will help you or someone around you.

Each spirit guide is unique just as each person is and each guide will give you feelings in different ways. Sometimes the signs or feelings from your spirit guides can feel so relaxed and easy that you may doubt what you are feeling.

There does not always have to be a large lightning bolt from the sky and a huge booming voice talking to you. Often your guides are just simple, quiet, nurturing presences who help you through very specific parts of your life. That is why they are called guides!

Types of spirit guides

From what I have experienced and learnt there are at least two different types of spirit guides that help you on your spiritual path: inner band guides and outer band guides.

Inner band guides

Your inner band guides are the spirit guides that help you regularly. They have the most to do with your spiritual development. Your inner band of guides is made up of the following guides.

» *Your main spirit guide who helps you from the moment you are conceived right up until you pass away back in spirit form. This is the guide you would receive the most information from and who you would usually feel the strongest when you work psychically.*

» *Your gatekeeper guide is a very important guide to have. This guide will protect your energy and act as a shield for you when you need psychic protection. Your gatekeeper guide is like a coffee filter; it sifts all of the negativity or psychic junk out through the filter so that only the clear good stuff can come through.*

It is very simple to meet your gatekeeper guide. All that you have to do is relax, close your eyes and ask in your mind for your gatekeeper guide to please come forward for you. You need to affirm to the Universe that you need your gatekeeper to be filled with the white light, full of love and for it to be very protective to keep all negativity away from you. You can use any words that suit you.

The next thing you can do is to imagine what your gatekeeper guide looks like. Think of the strongest, most powerful image of someone or something in your mind. For example, my gatekeeper guide looks like the big, tall African-American from the movie, *The Green Mile*. He is incredibly physically strong as well as beautifully compassionate and loving. I know of many people who choose to call upon Archangel Michael to be their gatekeeper guide.

It can help to have a visual image so that you can relate to your gatekeeper guide. If you ever feel scared or need extra help or protection call upon your gatekeeper guide or Archangel Michael.

Specialist guides are guides that are unique to you. All of us have a unique personality and purpose here on Earth, so each of your specialist guides need to match you in their individuality. I have a special guide who is like a psychic information guide in that she helps me to deliver information to people, like a channelling guide. I also have a creative guide who helps me to write my books. There are many different guides for all the different parts of my life. You may choose to only work with your main spirit guide who then operates as the go-between for you, communicating with the other guides on your behalf.

Outer band guides

Your outer band spirit guides are the guides that come and go in your life. They are with you for a specific reason and season. They may be a creative guide to help you with your creative work, a healing guide to help you through an illness, or a guide to help you with making changes in your life.

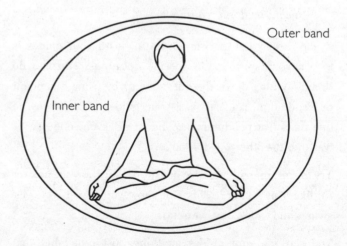

Ways to communicate with your spirit guides

> » *Dreaming (conscious daydreaming, conscious dreaming, lucid dreaming)*

> » *Past life regression (under hypnosis)*

> » *Scrying (bowl of black ink, glass of water, with a black mirror, crystal ball)*

> » *Pendulum (yes/no closed questions)*

> » *Meditation*

> » *Automatic writing*

> » *Psychic/medium reading.*

A good way to start communicating with your guides is to ask your spirit guide specific questions. You can do this by writing down the questions or by using a pendant or pendulum. You can ask your guides straight yes/no questions. The pendulum or pendant will swing one way for 'yes' and the other way for 'no'.

Try to start off with practice questions you know the answer to, like 'Am I male?' This will show you which way 'yes' swings and which way is for 'no'.

You can ask your guides anything, just remember that ultimately they are here to guide you in your life, not to make the decisions for you. It's not healthy to depend totally on your guides input, all the time; you still need to be able to have control over your own decisions.

When asking questions of your guides in your mind, always listen to the first answer you hear in your mind. The first answer is always your spirit guides; the second answer is you doubting yourself or second guessing.

EXERCISE TO FEEL YOUR SPIRIT GUIDES

Sit comfortably in a chair and place both feet on the floor. Relax. You may like to have your eyes closed when you do this exercise; do whatever is comfortable for you. Make sure you have psychically protected yourself with a shielding exercise such as the bubble or the cloak (see pp. 55–57).

When you are ready ask for your spirit guide to come forward. You can ask out loud or in your mind. Ask for your spirit guide to give you a physical sensation on your body so that you know that they are with you. Take note of the feelings you are experiencing; list them on the worksheet that follows.

Try not to be too hard on yourself if do not feel or sense your spirit guide at first, it can take practice.

Some spirit guides might not give you a physical sensation as they may prefer to show you things via another method of communication.

Do you feel any warmth or heat in an area of your body?

_____

_____

Or do you feel a coolness or shivery feeling on your body?

_____

_____

Is there any tingling?

_____

_____

Does the hair on your arms or back of your neck stand up?

_____

_____

How did you feel when you sensed your spirit guide with you?

_____

_____

You have more than one spirit guide. Each spirit guide is individual and will work with you in different ways. Once you have felt this spirit guide you can then go further to find out more about this guide. Once you are familiar with one guide you can repeat the process to meet your other guides as well.

Crystals to use to connect with your spirit guides

Angelite

Sodalite

Lapis lazuli

Clear quartz

Seraphinite

Larimar

Turquoise

Labradorite

Moonstone

Apophyllite

Petalite

Amethyst

Questions to ask your spirit guides

» *Are you of the light and do you bow before the Lord/Great Spirit/God/Goddess?*

» *Are you male or female?*

» *Are you my main guide?*

» *Are you around me often?*

» *Do I have more than just one guide? Do I have more than two guides, etc?*

» *Have we known each other before in previous lives?*

» *Am I on the right spiritual path?*

» *Will you please help me to get onto the right path for me spiritually?*

» *Can you please give me a feeling on my body so that I know when you are near?*

Here are a few examples of questions you can ask your guides if you wish to do automatic writing.

» *What is your name?*

» *What area do you guide me in?*

» *Do you have any special messages for me at the moment?*

» *Can you please show me a particular colour or symbol that represents you?*

» *Is there a special feeling or sensation that you can give me to represent you?*

» *Will you describe your appearance to me please?*

» *In your opinion would it best for me to do ....?*

» *What do I need to focus on the most at the moment?*

Meet your spirit guide meditation

This is a special meditation. Before you start you may want to prepare your meditation space in a special way. Make sure that you won't be disturbed. You may like to close the curtains or blinds, light a candle or burn some of your favourite incense to add to the atmosphere. This meditation will take around 15 minutes so you will need to find a comfortable position that you can retain for that amount of time.

It's important that you call upon your spirit guides, angels, god or goddesses, whichever feels right for you. Ask them to keep you protected in the white light. See yourself surrounded by a bubble of bright white light and know that you are protected at all times in this meditation, and if you wish to return to the present you can do so at any time.

During this meditation relax and take your time. Try to imagine as much detail as possible. Go with the flow with what you see or experience and keep your thoughts relaxed. Try not to go into this meditation with any preconceived ideas of what you will find.

 ## SPIRIT GUIDE MEDITATION

Please get into a position where you can feel very relaxed. You can sit in a position that is the most comfortable for you, or if you want to stretch out and lie down on the floor, that is fine as well.

Close your eyes and take a deep breath in. As you breathe out let go of any worry or anxiety, try to let these things float from your mind. Breathe in slowly and exhale slowly, breathe in again and exhale slowly. Relax and feel yourself letting go of all your thoughts.

Start to feel your body relaxing. It is a comfortable feeling. Your back is supported by the chair. Your feet are touching the floor. Your arms are relaxed in your lap. If you are lying on the floor you will feel supported by the floor. Feel your back relaxing, your arms and legs are feeling lighter and lighter, your head is relaxed.

Now focus your attention on your breathing. Notice how steady and relaxed it is. It is like a steady beat. First breathe in, breathe out. As you breathe in, see a beautiful white energy filling your lungs. As you breathe out, see your troubles, worries and problems leave you.

When you are ready, visualise yourself standing in the middle of a beautiful lush, green forest. Breathe in the cool moist air. Notice that there is a fine mist surrounding you.

Take a few moments to get your bearings, notice that you can hear a soft bird call far away in the distance. The mist starts to clear now.

You look down and you notice that there is an ancient stone pathway leading into the distance. You take a deep breath in and decide to begin to follow the path.

As you walk along the pathway you begin to count your steps — 1, 2, 3, feel the hard ancient stones beneath your feet; 4, 5, 6, a soft, green tree fern brushes your leg as you walk past, 7, 8, 9.

You begin to hear drumming in the distance, you stop and listen. Your heart starts to pound with excitement as you realise that you are on the right path to meeting your spirit guide.

The pathway leads to a large open field with patches of tiny yellow and white daisies scattered everywhere. The sun is shining brightly and it warms your face.

Take in a deep breath and feel relaxed as you sit down on the lush green grass. This is your special sanctuary; you can come here at any time to meet your spirit guide or just to relax. You are completely safe, nothing can harm you here.

When you are ready it is time for you to ask for your spirit guide to come forward to meet with you. Please do not be afraid, you have known your spirit guide for many lifetimes; your spirit guide will never do anything to harm you.

As you wait for your spirit guide to arrive you notice that the beating of the drum is getting louder and louder, it matches your own heartbeat.

Out of the corner of your eye you start to notice a bright light coming towards you. The drumming begins to fade, you breathe easily.

As the light moves closer and closer to you, you realise that this is your spirit guide. When you are ready you can invite your spirit guide to join you. Your heart fills with love as the light disappears and your spirit guide appears in front of you. You both sit down facing each other in the meadow to reconnect.

Take a moment to see what your spirit guide looks like.

Is your spirit guide wearing any significant clothes, hats or feathers?

Is your spirit guide a male or female?

This is your chance to ask your spirit guide anything that you would like to know.

You may like to ask your spirit guide if you have known them in a previous life.

You can ask if you are on the right path this lifetime or if they can show you a symbol of something that you need or something you need to work on.

I will leave you for a few moments to talk with your spirit guide.

As you talk with your spirit guide know that you can meet them at any time, they are always with you.

Finally, ask your spirit guide for a physical feeling on your body so that you know it is your spirit guide and this will be their confirmation for you.

The sun is beginning to set now, the time has come for you to say goodbye to your spirit guide. You both rise to your feet, your spirit guide pulls you close to give you a hug goodbye.

Please thank your spirit guide for coming to meet with you today. As you thank your spirit guide you notice that the drumming has begun again in the distance.

You look up at your spirit guide and see that a bright white light has surrounded your guide once more. The bright light with your spirit guide in it moves back into the distance towards the drumming.

It's time now for you to walk out of the open field and to head back along the stone path.

As you walk along the path you begin to feel the coolness of the forest and you count your steps — 10, 9, 8, the light is getting dimmer as you move further back through the forest; 7, 6, 5, a bird calls softly to its mate in the distance; 4, 3, the mist is coming in now; 2, 1. The mist starts to fade away and you begin to become aware of your surroundings.

Bring your awareness back now slowly. Keeping your eyes closed for a moment, start to wiggle your toes and fingers. Now stretch your arms up above your head. You can open your eyes and realise now that you are back in the safety of your room. You are in your current life and you do not have to hold onto anything that has hurt you or held you back in your past life.

It's very important that you write down everything you have seen, felt or experienced before you forget what has happened.

The final thing you should do is have a glass of water and something grounding to eat, to make sure that you have brought your complete awareness back and have grounded your energy.

Thank you for going on this journey, remember you can communicate with your spirit guide anytime, anywhere.

ANGELS

Are angels real? Yes, angels are real. Angels have been documented since man first began to communicate, whether through art, writing, dance or the spoken word. Angels have been sighted and felt psychically or energetically by people of all ages, ethnicity, religions and belief systems. It can be hard to believe that they exist if you haven't experienced them yourself or been in contact with someone who is aware of angels at work in their life.

There are many specific angels and archangels to call upon for different tasks. If you would like to find out more about angels, you can find various books that specialise in all things angelic.

The hospital angels

I have experienced a few very special encounters with angels but mostly I like to work with my spirit guides for the more earthly concerns. However, I will call upon angels for specific things when I am in need of some extra special healing for myself or my loved ones.

I remember when my second child Zane was a baby, he would have been only around six to nine months of age. He had very high temperatures and was rushed to the Children's Hospital. I was sitting with him in the emergency room and the doctors told me that he had a bad case of pneumonia. At that time I knew that I needed to call upon the highest help of all to help my little baby. I sat down next to his cot in the emergency room, closed my eyes and silently called for help from the angels. I asked them to please come to help heal my little boy. I imagined surrounding him in the white light but as hard as I could, I couldn't see it because I was so stressed and worried about him. It was a very scary time and he was so sick, he could barely breathe.

My husband was at home with our other little boy and had called family members to ask for help and to let them know. As I sat there crying by myself with him in the cot, I felt a great warmth spread throughout my body. I looked up at his cot and saw the most amazing thing.

Surrounding his cot were the tallest pillars of light I have ever seen. I could not see any faces, just tall white lights and as I looked closer I saw the outlines of wings. They were not like you see in traditional paintings or statues. The outlines were so bright. This vision lasted for only the briefest time, possibly only a few seconds, but it felt like a lot longer. While writing this I can still see what it looked like and I can still feel the heat and warmth from the angels.

It doesn't end there though, it gets better. At that stage of my life many of my family members were still unaware of my spiritual path. I didn't want to tell them what I had experienced. I didn't want anyone to doubt or put any negativity on such a beautiful personal experience. The most amazing thing is later that day one of my older brothers, Matt called me up to check on Zane. He said he was so worried about him that he had tried to send him healing. This older brother of mine was already on his spiritual path and is a healer. He then went on to tell me that the most amazing thing happened to him when he was focusing on Zane.

He told me that he had seen a bright light around Zane and there were at least six to seven angels surrounding his cot. I burst into tears and told him I had seen the same thing. We could not believe it. My brother had seen this in his mind clairvoyantly at his home and I had seen it with my physical eyes in the hospital at exactly the same time. This was a big confirmation to us that angels are real and that the power of love and hope does indeed work.

Thank you to the angels that day as they did save my son and he was healthy and out of hospital within a few days.

This is just one of the experiences I have had. There are too many to list, but I hear stories like this every day about angels or spirits coming to help at just the right time in accidents, or in time to protect or stop something from happening.

Common questions about angels

Is my passed loved one my guardian angel?

It depends on what your own belief systems are and what your definition of the term 'guardian angel' is. My understanding is that guardian angels are separate from your passed loved ones. Most angels have not actually lived on the Earth and had the dense earthly experience. The term guardian angel can sometimes be confusing because some people call their spirit guides their guardian angel.

Your passed loved ones can definitely still look after you and guide you, but they are not the same high pure vibration as an angel. It is totally up to you what you want to call your passed loved ones; the term 'guardian angel' may give you some relief or make sense to you.

What is the difference between angels and spirit guides?

Most angels have not had a physical life on Earth. They are pure spirit beings who are made up of a very high energy vibration and who have not been tainted by the earthly trials and tribulations that we all go through as humans. They have very specific tasks to perform.

Spirit guides also have specific tasks, but they come from a place of empathy; they know what it is like to have been human because they have experienced many lifetimes on Earth.

Ghosts/ earthbound spirits

A ghost is the common name used for an earthbound spirit. Ghosts are spirits that are still attached energetically to particular places like their homes, to objects such as jewellery or to people such as their family members.

Ghosts have been given bad publicity over the years and have been feared by both adults and children. The reason these spirits are earthbound is because they have not chosen to go to the light and enter the next energy phase out of fear, confusion or attachment to the physical world. The energy around ghosts can sometimes feel very heavy, confused or even frightened, and it is this that can be perceived as being negative.

In my experience, ghosts — or earthbound spirits as I like to call them — are like lost children wanting to go home. You cannot blame them for being confused or not understanding why no one can hear or see them. They need help to be shown to the light so that they can be happy and move on spiritually.

Male ghost in a function room

Recently I was teaching a group of students over a weekend away in the mountains. We were booked in to use a particular function room, but when we arrived we were informed that our function room had been converted into a restaurant. We were shown to another function room. I thought nothing of this change as it was to a bigger, brighter room that actually suited us better.

Later on that first day after lunch I was talking to one of the staff members of the resort. He asked me what my conference was about. I told him it was about psychic development and I went on to tell him that I was a psychic medium. He was very interested. He quietly asked me if I could talk to him for a moment away from the group.

I went with him, wondering what was going on. He told me that he and the other staff members were worried that there was a ghost at the resort. I asked him where they felt it the most. He said that the room that I was meant to be using for my conference was the function room that everyone felt scared to be in.

I thought this was so typical of spirit, to send me to a place which is haunted. What a great lesson this was to be for my students. I went with the man and went into the previous function room. As soon as I walked into the dark room I could feel a male presence there. He was very angry and had a very old-fashioned feeling about him. He was not happy being disturbed. I quickly looked around the room and walked back outside with the male staff member.

I asked him what had happened to other staff members, what had they felt. He said that the staff were scared in this room, many of them felt like someone was watching them. A female staff member had lit the room with candles for a function; the function had been very successful. After the function was over she went in and cleared the tables and blew the candles out. She then went and took some things out to the kitchen and came back in and all the candles had been relit. No one else was around that area to light them. Let's just say she was freaked out. The male staff member went on to say that other staff had experienced books coming out of the bookshelf at them as they walked past the fireplace.

I asked him if he wanted me to try and work with this spirit or move it on. I said that he would have to get permission from the owners of the resort as it needed to be ok with them. He said he would get back to me about it.

I then went back to the lunch table and quietly told Richard, my manager, about this. He said not to let anyone know as it may freak the students out. We should tell them at the end of the weekend so that they wouldn't be scared.

On the last day the male staff member gave me the ok from the owners to work with the spirit to move it on. I decided to wait until after lunch. I told my students that I had a little surprise exercise for them to do. I told them that it might not suit everyone and if they didn't want to they didn't have to join in because it would involve working with spirit energy that might be a bit angry.

All of the students wanted to come. The male staff member let us into the room and I asked him not to tell the students anything. I wanted them to sense things themselves first. We walked in. Instantly the room felt heavy, dark and angry.

I asked my students to see if they felt anything. They all said they did and most of them said they felt a male energy that was angry. A few said they felt a second spirit, a female spirit, in the other corner as well.

Most of them pointed to the bookcase and fireplace where I had felt him as well. A couple of them were getting quite scared. I asked the students if they wanted to stay and help remove the spirit or they could go and have some fresh air and meet up with us later. They still all decided to stay.

This was something I had not planned in my lesson plan for the weekend, but it was so beneficial for them to learn it firsthand.

To begin with, I went around to each corner of the room with my protection spray spritzer and I asked for all negativity to be removed and for protection for myself and the students and the accompanying staff member. In my mind I called upon my gatekeeper and spirit guides to come forward. I asked my students to do the same thing with their guides. I then asked for them to all imagine the white light around themselves and the whole property.

We all held hands in the circle. I lit three candles and placed them in the centre of the circle. I asked the students to focus on the candles and we all tried to encourage him to go to the white light, by asking him to go to the light. He was very angry and would not leave. I told the students to keep the circle together, not to let go of anyone's hands. It was important to stay strong. I then called upon Archangel Michael and imagined a big pair of white hands coming to take this spirit to the light. I told the students to say three times, 'It's time to go to the white light in love'. We all chanted this three times. As we said this I felt a heat come over me and then I saw a red light out of the corner of my eye.

Immediately, the energy was a lot calmer and cooler. I told the students to let out a deep breath. They were all amazed at what they had experienced. It was important to tell them to snuff out the candles, not to blow it out. The reason I snuff the candle, out is to make sure that the energy has been released.

Sending this spirit to the light does not harm it in any way; it is a way to help it to grow spiritually. He was stuck in that room. He felt that he still belonged to the area and was getting disturbed by the constant stream of people in and out of the restaurant. His energy had been trapped there for a very long time.

The resort was built on a big piece of land that was traditional farming land. He may have been one of the drovers or one of the original landowners. He was now free to connect with his loved ones in spirit and to move on spiritually without being stuck earthbound. The owners and staff of the resort are now happy to work in that area.

GODS AND GODDESSES

There are many specific Gods and Goddesses from many different cultures that people like to call upon for help with specific things. Each God or Goddess has a specific purpose or strength. When I work psychically I do not channel any Gods or Goddesses I choose to work mainly with my spirit guides, but I do like to call upon particular Gods or Goddesses when I need help with something. I like to call on the Hindu God Ganesh (also pronounced Ganesha) who is the God of wisdom and remover of obstacles to remove all obstacles around me when I feel blocked or need to move through something quickly. Ganesh is the elephant god with many arms. There is a lot of information available on the internet or in books about all of the different Gods and Goddesses.

WHO ARE YOU WORKING WITH IN SPIRIT?

As you can see there are various types of spirit entities that you may come in contact with or will connect with when you are opening yourself up psychically to the spiritual world. Just as I have discussed earlier there are positive high vibration spirits and lower vibration negative spirits out there in the spiritual world. It is very important that you know who you are working with in spirit. You can choose to work with whatever energy resonates the best for you.

It's also very important to know who or what you are working with psychically so that you are not fed incorrect information and also so that you can work with the right energy when you need to. For example, if you want to call upon a particular guide or god or goddess to help you with writing or creativity, you would focus on that energy.

When you learn to connect with your own spirit guides you will eventually be able to tell who you are working with and what kind of spirit energy you are dealing with.

 ## WHO ARE YOU WORKING WITH SPIRIT EXERCISE

The following exercise is designed to help you to understand who and what you are working with in spirit. Be as honest as possible when answering the questions. Remember to write down your first answer as it is often the right answer, the second thing you think of can sometimes be you doubting yourself.

How do you think you sense your spirit guides? Is it a physical feeling such as heat, cold or tingles, or do you hear or smell them?

_____

_____

_____

Where can you feel the spirit energy, for example, around your head height, shoulders or down near your knees?

_____

_____

_____

Identify what kind of spirit you are with or communicating with. Do you think it is an animal spirit guide, a spirit guide, an angel, or a passed loved one? How have you identified what kind of spirit it is?

_____

_____

_____

Does the energy feel positive or negative to you? How does it make you feel emotionally?

_____

_____

_____

Does the spirit feel like it is a male or female energy? Or does it feel like it is just a spirit form which is not male or female?

_____

_____

_____

If this feels like a passed loved one or a deceased spirit trying to connect with you, ask them if they can give you specific information to say who they are, such as an age group — are they older or younger or the same generation as you? Are they related to you or do they just want to deliver a message to you?

_____

_____

_____

_____

When working with the passed loved one you can also ask if they have any significant physical characteristics, or they may like to tell you a name or a date that relates to them.

_____

_____

_____

Remember to leave the message as it is, say it exactly as you see it. Sometimes it won't make sense to you but it may make sense to someone else or to you at a later date.

_____

_____

_____

Is it real or am I just crazy?

The hardest thing to come to terms with when you are starting out on your spiritual path is if you are really hearing things from spirit or if you are making things up. A lot of people who come to see me either for readings or for my workshops ask the same question. They ask the following questions: Am I going nuts? Am I schizophrenic? Have I read too many spiritual books or seen too many paranormal TV shows?

The easy answer to these questions is no you are not going nuts (yes, there are some people who have paranoia or real mental health issues so you should check that out if you feel it could very well be a problem for you). But usually most people do feel, hear and sense things that are, in fact, messages from their spirit guides, passed loved ones or their own intuition.

There is no quick way to become confident in your psychic ability. It takes many years and many confirmations to get to a place in your mind or spiritual self that you know you can trust that it is indeed spirit, not you. Yes there are people who are naturally gifted psychics and mediums who take to their spiritual gifts very easily, but even these people — and I am one of them — have to take years to understand who and what they are working with and how to distinguish between different spirits and signs.

Just as most of us are born with the ability to learn to crawl, then walk and then run as we grow up, everyone is born with their own sixth sense or intuition. Some people will learn as they grow how to run faster than others, through practice, determination, the correct diet and exercise and, yes, having the right genetic make-up helps as well. Not everyone who wants to be a professional runner will always make the Olympics, but many will do well at a state, or local level or even just run for enjoyment.

The same applies with psychic gifts. Not everyone has to be a professional psychic or medium. Everyone has their own special abilities and gifts. Try not to feel pressure that you must have a certain type of spiritual gift, such as being a reiki master or a psychic medium. There does not have to be labels on your gifts and you do not have to have a wall full of certificates to prove that you are connected with spirit.

I remember when I first started wanting to do readings for the general public. I was terrified about how I was going to prove who I was and how I could connect with spirit. I knew that I could do accurate readings as I had done so over many years, but when it came to having to prove what I could do for strangers it was a daunting task.

I was talking to my friend/mentor Lilbearpawwoman on the phone one day many years ago; she was in the United States and I was in Australia. I told her of my concerns, that

I didn't have a degree or a piece of paper that I could show my potential clients. She listened to my concerns and said to me, 'Jade, you don't need pieces of paper to say who you are or what your gifts are'. I tried to explain to her that in Australia a lot of people went to courses or did reiki training and did, in fact, carry a lot of pieces of paper or certificates to prove what they had learnt.

She laughed at me about this. Lilbearpawwoman said to me that it was ok for them to have that if they wished but I did not need to do such a thing. And she was right! So I say the same thing to you now, please don't put a label on your psychic ability. Each person has their own psychic gifts or intuition. None is better than the other; each is just as special and different.

I hope that you have learnt more about your own intuition and now have the skills to reconnect with your spirit guides. May you continue to enjoy working on your psychic development and may you have a sense of peace and fulfilment in knowing that you are not alone. You have many helpers in the spirit world who are there to make your life happier and easier.

Many blessings to you and your family as you journey through life,

Jade-Sky x

NOTES

The No Excuses Guide to Soul Mates
Create an exciting action plan to attract the
relationship you desire quickly & easily;
The Ideal Partner Shopping list; Identify
Deal breakers & Negotiable points with
your Soul Mate.
*Co-authored by Stacey Demarco
and Jade-Sky.*

ISBN: 9782921295218

What Happens Next?
Spiritual medium Jade-Sky shows that it
is possible to feel, sense or even hear your
passed loved ones in spirit.
Jade-Sky is asked hundreds of questions
about life after death and here she
answers them all: What happens to loved
ones when they pass; How to recognise
signs from passed loved ones; and What
are angels, spirit guides and ghosts?

ISBN 9781921295324

**What Happens Next?
Inspiration Cards**
Jade-Sky's *What Happens Next
Inspiration Cards* are a beautiful
44 deck of cards that will enable you
to connect with your spirit guides
and angels. Assisted with a booklet
on how to use the cards, they will give
you the answers you need and help
guide you past any obstacles that life
throws your way.

ISBN: 9781921878039

Available in all good bookstores and online at
www.rockpoolpublishing.com.au.